DIVINE REFLECTIONS

Divine Reflections

A Journey Through Faith, Wisdom, and Love

DR. ANNA LIGHTFOOT-WARD

Johnathan Lightfoot

CLN Publishing

Contents

Chapter 1

A Tree of Life

Proverbs 15:4

Where there is openness, honesty, and common sense, there is a tree of life; a path to oneness with God. When we are one with God, the true reality is without confusion about God's expectations of us in our daily walk-through time. The reality is that God wants only what is good for us. This alone ought to be our compass in life.

Conversely, perverseness is one's purposeful inclination to be unreasonably stubborn, contrary, or willfully persistent in what is wrong. To know to do what is right and righteous and not do is perverseness and a breach in one's own spirit with God. The right path is one of openness, honesty, and common sense; for these are the true reality.

To have a breach in spirit speaks to a separation from the true reality and a mindset toward one's own reality; a reality that vacates openness, honesty, and common sense. These qualities are natural to us. However, and because "darkness" is ever present to haunt and hurt, we experience vulnerability. The feeling of vulnerability is a confused state of mind, one that continues to focus on the hurt that is a reality different from God's purpose, and a breach in the spirit with Him.

Therefore, it is better that a breach in the spirit be completely avoided, as an eternal trust in the all-knowing and seeing God will bind wounds, vindicate right, and keep the peace for those who are a tree of life.

Introduction: The Journey to Spiritual Wholeness

Imagine standing at the base of an ancient, towering tree, its branches stretching towards the sky, offering a sense of security and wisdom. This tree represents the spiritual path we embark upon when we embrace the transformative power of openness, honesty, and common sense. This chapter will delve into the profound wisdom hidden within Proverbs 15:4, guiding you on a journey of self-discovery and spiritual growth. Together, we will uncover the secrets of the tree Tree of Life and perils of perverseness, ultimately learning how to align our souls with the Divine and navigate the complexities of our spiritual lives with grace and clarity.

Proverbs 15:4 (KJV): "A wholesome tongue is a tree of life: but perverseness therein is a breach in the spirit."

With this verse as our foundation, let's begin our exploration of the tree of life and the consequences of perverseness in our spiritual journey.

The Tree of Life
Original Text:
Where there is openness, honesty, and common sense, there is a tree of life; a path to oneness with God. When we are one with God, the true reality is without confusion about God's expectations of us in our daily walk-through time. The reality is that God wants only what is good for us. This alone ought to be our compass in life.

Commentary:
The tree of life symbolizes the spiritual journey we embark upon when we embrace openness, honesty, and common sense. This path leads to a deep connection with God and allows us to understand His expectations for our lives, guiding us toward what is truly good and beneficial.

Reflection Question:
How has embracing openness, honesty, and common sense brought you closer to oneness with God?

The Pitfalls of Perverseness
Original Text:
Conversely, perverseness is one's purposeful inclination to be unreasonably stubborn, contrary, or willfully persistent in what is wrong. To know to do what is right and righteous and not do is perverseness and a breach in one's own spirit with God The right path is one of openness, honesty, and common sense; for these are the true reality.

Commentary:
Perverseness involves deliberately choosing to act in a stubborn, contrary manner, and persisting in doing what is wrong. This attitude creates a breach in our spirit and distances us from God. The true path, which is aligned with openness,

honesty, and common sense, is the one we must follow to remain connected with the Divine.

Reflection Question:

Can you recall a time when you knowingly chose a path of perverseness? What were the consequences, and how did it affect your relationship with God?

A Breach in Spirit: Separation from True Reality

Original Text:

To have a breach in spirit speaks to a separation from the true reality and a mindset toward one's own reality; a reality that vacates openness, honesty, and common sense. These qualities are natural to us. However, and because "darkness" is ever present to haunt and hurt, we experience vulnerability. The feeling of vulnerability is a confused state of mind, one that continues to focus on the hurt that is a reality different from God's purpose, and a breach in the spirit with Him.

Commentary:

Having a breach in our spirit signifies a separation from the true reality, leading us to create our own distorted version of it. This alternate reality abandons the principles of openness, honesty, and common sense. Although these values are innate to us, the ever-present darkness threatens to harm and mislead us, leaving us vulnerable. Vulnerability is a state of confusion and preoccupation and with pain, distances us from God's purpose and severs our spiritual connection with Him.

Reflection Question:

How can you recognize when you are drifting away from the true reality and moving towards a mindset that lacks openness, honesty, and common sense? What steps can you take to realign yourself with God's purpose?

Healing and Peace through Trust in God
Original Text:
Therefore, it is better that a breach in the spirit be completely avoided, as an eternal trust in the all-knowing and seeing God will bind wounds, vindicate right, and keep the peace for those who are a tree of life.

Commentary:
To maintain a strong connection with God, it is essential to avoid breaching our spirit. Placing our eternal trust in the all-knowing and ever-present God enables us to heal our wounds, find vindication, and maintain inner peace. By choosing to be a tree of life, we embrace the path of openness, honesty, and common sense, nurturing our relationship with the Divine.

Reflection Question:
In what ways can you cultivate trust in the all-knowing and ever-present God to help you maintain a strong spiritual connection and inner peace?

Conclusion: Embracing the Path to Spiritual Enlightenment

Our journey through the insights of Proverbs 15:4 has illu-
minated the significance of openness, honesty, and common
sense as cornerstones of our spiritual journey. As we've pon-
dered the wisdom found in Dr. Lightfoot-Ward's **Original Text**,
we've gained a deeper understanding of the tree of life and the
dangers of perverseness. By actively applying these lessons to
our daily lives, we forge a stronger spiritual connection and
nurture our personal growth, ultimately moving closer to oneness with God.

As we continue our exploration in the next chapter, "Toward the End," we'll delve into the importance of maintaining
focus on our spiritual goals and remaining steadfast in our pursuit of enlightenment. Join us on this transformative journey
as we uncover the hidden treasures that await us on our path
to spiritual wholeness.

Chapter 2

Toward the End

1 John 2:16

For all that is in the world is not of God but of the world, a world fleeting and without permanence in the realm of certainty.

When a person's focus is on satisfying one's own desires, these desires are not of God but of the world, the physical world. The reality of life will find desires to be illusions. That which is spiritual is the true reality; the failing is in man confusing the senses by cleaving to sensual things rather than to God.

Even more remarkable is that the end of sensual things causes hurt and further confusion. The cycle engaged therewith is never ending, until vanity showcases purpose as the essence of life, its plight generally left undone.

It is not a hard thing to know the locus of one's heart. If energy spent focuses on material things, immediate gratification, and laudable applause, the focus is worldly and of the world. When finally understood that one's life is at an end, the compass toward God is too long vacated, and the pause that is time, is completed.

Introduction: Toward the End

As we continue on our spiritual journey, we encounter the challenge of balancing our earthly desires with our pursuit of spiritual growth. In this chapter titled "Toward the End," we will delve into the wisdom found in 1 John 2:16, exploring the distinction between what is of God and what is of the world. By understanding the impermanence of worldly desires and the importance of focusing on our spiritual development, we can guide our hearts toward a deeper connection with the Divine and navigate life's journey with a sense of purpose and clarity.

1 John 2:16 (KJV):

"For all that is in the world, the lust of the flesh, eyes, and the pride of life, is not of the Father, but is of the world."

Let us now examine the insights on this verse and reflect upon the implications for our own spiritual growth.

Original Text:
For all that is in the world is not of God but of the world, a world fleeting and without permanence in the realm of certainty.

Commentary:
Here, we are reminded that worldly desires, which are not of God, can be fleeting and uncertain. It is important to recognize that our focus should be on the spiritual realm, which offers a sense of certainty and permanence.

Reflective Question:
Are there areas in your life where you might be placing too much emphasis on worldly desires, rather than shifting your focus toward spiritual growth?

Original Text:
When a person's focus is on satisfying one's own desires, these desires are not of God but of the physical world. The reality of life will find desires to be illusions. That which is spiritual is the true reality; the failing is in man confusing the senses by cleaving to sensual things rather than to God.

Commentary:
Focusing on satisfying our own desires can lead us into a cycle of hurt and confusion. The emphasis here is that the spiritual realm is the true reality, and our struggles arise when we become too attached to sensual things instead of seeking God.

Reflective Question:
What steps can you take to cultivate a deeper spiritual connection and avoid the pitfalls of attachment to sensual desires?

Original Text:

It is not a hard thing to know the locus of one's heart. If energy spent focuses on material things, immediate gratification, and laudable applause, the focus is worldly and of the world. When finally understood that one's life is at an end, the compass toward God is too long vacated, and unfortunately, the pause of time, is completed.

Commentary:

We are encouraged to examine our hearts and evaluate where our focus truly lies. If we find that our energy is spent on material things and immediate gratification, we must redirect our focus toward God and his desire for our spiritual growth.

Reflective Question:

In what ways can you adjust your priorities to ensure your heart's focus is aligned with your spiritual journey and growth?

Conclusion: Embracing Spiritual Priorities

In our exploration of 1 John 2:16, we've gained valuable insights into the importance of distinguishing between worldly desires and spiritual pursuits. As we reflect on the wisdom shared in this chapter titled "Toward the End," we can learn to navigate life's journey with a spiritual focus, ensuring that our heart remains aligned with our path to the Divine. As we continue our journey into the next chapter, "Working Together for the Good," let us remember the lessons learned here and embrace the spiritual priorities that will guide us forward.

Chapter 3

Working Together
for the Good

Jeremiah 33:3

"The promises of Allah are always uplifting and beyond what anyone can imagine. The "threes" in the above verse are very interesting, and the action and result are exceptionally profound. How often is it that we call upon God with our questions, concerns, wonderings, and more basically, with a need for answers? Here we find Allah beseeching us to direct our thoughts, minds, heart, soul, and strength toward Him. He desires and wants us to know that He will answer. Beyond a simple answer, however, Allah further assures that with the answer will come great and mighty things, of which we do not have knowledge. In other words, the response will be more than the inquiry. For we do not know what to ask, He, however, certainly knows how to answer.

I'm often reminded of how sales calls tend to be limited in scope and reference. The salesperson's job is to present only a small view, and yet the commitment is a larger obligation from the buyer than initially intended. The bottom line being the key and the higher the bottom line, the better. This is generally called a "blind" purchase wherein the seller introduces a product, a potential buyer shows interest, and a transaction is commenced for purchase. At the juncture, the seller prods the consumer to purchase more, and the consumer thinks the "deal" is a bargain becomes a partner in the transaction and many of the add-ons. The result is the "product, to which more is sold, and the seller leaves content in having proved the aggressor in the transaction, the consumer being "hoodwinked" by the product and/or the cost of the product.

Allah does not operate in such a matter. When we have concerns, He not only answers the concern but through divine revelation, shows us the many "angles" involved in the concern. In other words, we become knowledgeable beyond the obvious and content to understand the "bigger" picture rather than the situational circumstances. Thus, when viewed panoramically, the true perspective is focused, and our ability to refocus, release and relax proves inviting.

Finally, it is the "which thou knowest not" that blesses me even more in this verse. I may approach Allah one-dimensionally, but His response will be multidimensional and beyond what I could ever imagine. Even so, it is how I handle the response that speaks volumes to my faith, trust, and hopes in His plan for my life. The ultimate dividend being all things working together for my good. Glory Hallelujah!!!"

Introduction: Working Together for the Good

In this chapter titled "Working Together for the Good," we explore the uplifting promises of Allah found in Jeremiah 33:3. This verse presents an interesting use of the number three and highlights the profound action and result that follow. We often turn to God with our questions, concerns, and wonderings, seeking answers and guidance. Allah calls us to direct our thoughts, minds, hearts, souls, and strength toward Him, promising not only an answer but also great and mighty things that we could not have imagined. Allah's response is more than just an answer to our inquiry, as He knows what we need before we even ask.

Jeremiah 33:3 (KJV):

"Call unto me, and I will answer thee, and shew thee great and mighty things, which thou knowest not."

Original Text:

I'm often reminded of how sales calls tend to be limited in scope and reference. The salesperson's job is to present only a small view and yet commitment is a larger obligation from the buyer than initially intended; the bottom line being the key and the higher the bottom line, the better. This is generally called a "blind" purchase wherein the seller introduces a product, a potential buyer shows interest, and a transaction is commenced for purchase. At the juncture, the seller prods the consumer to purchase more; the consumer thinks the "deal" is a bargain becomes partner to the transaction and many of the add-ons. The result is the product, and more are sold; the seller leaves content in having proved the aggressor in the transaction, the consumer being "hoodwinked" by the product and/or the cost of the product.

Commentary:

Human perspective is often limited in scope and reference, as exemplified by sales calls that present only a small view of the product or service being sold. The salesperson's goal is to maximize the bottom line and persuade the buyer to commit to a larger obligation than initially intended, resulting in a "blind" purchase with the potential for hidden costs and add-ons. This highlights the importance of seeking guidance from Allah, who can provide us with knowledge beyond the obvious and help us see the bigger picture.

Reflective Question:

In what areas of your life do you feel limited by your perspective, and how can you seek guidance from Allah to broaden your understanding?

Original Text:

Allah does not operate in such a matter. When we have concerns, He not only answers the concern but through divine revelation, shows us the many "angles" involved in the concern. In other words, we become knowledgeable beyond the obvious and content to understand the "bigger" picture rather than the situational circumstances. Thus, when viewed panoramically, the true perspective is focused and our ability to refocus, release, and relax proves inviting.

Commentary:

Unlike salespeople who present limited information, Allah provides divine revelation that can show us the many angles involved in our concerns. This helps us become knowledgeable beyond the obvious and understand the bigger picture, allowing us to see beyond situational circumstances and gain a panoramic view of our lives. This broader perspective can help us refocus, release, and relax.

Reflective Question:

In what ways can you seek divine revelation and broaden your understanding of the bigger picture in your life?

Original Text:

Finally, it is the "which thou knowest not" that blesses me even more in this verse. I may approach Allah one-dimensionally, but His response will be multidimensional and beyond what I could ever imagine. Even so, it is how I handle the response that speaks volumes to my faith, trust, and hopes in His plan for my life; the ultimate dividend being all things working together for my good. Glory Hallelujah!!!

Commentary:

This verse highlights the fact that Allah's response to our prayers is multidimensional and beyond what we could ever imagine. It is our faith, trust, and hope in His plan for our lives and how we handle His response that determines the ultimate dividend - all things working together for our good.

Reflective Question:

How can you trust in Allah's plan for your life and believe that all things are working together for your good, even when His response to your prayers may not be what you expected or wanted?

Conclusion: The Multidimensional Blessings of Allah's Promises

The promises of Allah are indeed uplifting and beyond what anyone can imagine. In this chapter, we have explored how Allah's promises are multidimensional and how He can provide us with knowledge beyond the obvious. Through divine revelation, Allah can help us see the bigger picture and gain a panoramic view of our lives, refocusing our attention and helping us relax. It is our faith, trust, and hope in Allah's plan for our lives that determine the ultimate dividend - all things working together for our good. In the next chapter, "You Will or Thine Will," we will explore the importance of submitting our will to Allah and trusting in His plan for our lives, even when it may not align with our own desires.

Chapter 4

Your Will or
Thine Will

Psalm 25:22

At first glance of the presented Psalm, the verse appears as a needed request for Israel, who is the promise through which God "Hashem" determined His plan of salvation; its' genesis being a plea for or from a people who have failed to obey Hashem.

To redeem is to restore one to an original position of prestige. More clearly stated, it is the act of making something acceptable or pleasant in spite of its negative qualities or aspects or to restore to favor where there has been a failure.

The lesson is clear that disobedience results in failure and deprives one of a position of favor; the exchanged position is the condition of distress, anxiety, or danger. These troubles are the source or cause of mental suffering, nervousness, agitation, or shame about or for something that is happening or anticipated and include those things that expose or lend vulnerability to harm, injury, or loss.

While Hashem has made provisions for failure, the constant plea for redemption is a character flaw that expresses more the desire to do one's own will rather than the will of Hashem.

Introduction: Your Will or Thine Will

In this chapter titled "Your Will or Thine Will," we explore Psalm 25:22 and its relevance to our lives as believers. At first glance, the verse appears to be a plea from the people of Israel, who have failed to obey God and need redemption. However, the lesson goes deeper and highlights the consequences of disobedience and the importance of submitting to God's will.

Psalm 25:22 (KJV):

"Redeem Israel, O God, out of all his troubles."

Original Text:

At first glance of the presented Psalm, the verse appears as a needed request for Israel, who is the promise through which God Hashem determined His plan of salvation; its' genesis being a plea for or from a people who have failed to obey Hashem. To redeem is to restore one to an original position of prestige. More clearly stated, it is the act of making something acceptable or pleasant in spite of its negative qualities or aspects or to restore to favor where there has been a failure. The lesson is clear that disobedience results in failure and deprives one of a position of favor; the exchanged position is the condition of distress, anxiety, or danger. These troubles are the source or cause of mental suffering, nervousness, agitation, or shame about or for something that is happening or anticipated and include those things that expose or lend vulnerability to harm, injury, or loss.

Commentary:

The verse in Psalm 25:22 highlights the consequences of disobedience and the need for redemption. When we fail to obey God, we lose our position of favor and become vulnerable to distress, anxiety, and danger. These troubles can cause mental suffering, nervousness, agitation, and shame. Redemption, on the other hand, is the act of restoring us to our original position of prestige and making us acceptable and pleasant despite our negative qualities or aspects.

Reflective Question:

In what areas of your life do you struggle with disobedience, and how has it affected your position of favor with God?

Original Text:

While Hashem has made provisions for failure, the constant plea for redemption is a character flaw that expresses more the desire to do one's own will rather than the will of Hashem.

Commentary:

While God has made provisions for our failures, constantly pleading for redemption can be a character flaw that reveals a desire to do our own will rather than submit to God's will. We must learn to trust in God's plan for our lives and seek His will rather than our own.

Reflective Question:

In what ways can you better submit to God's will and trust in His plan for your life?

Conclusion: Your Will or Thine Will

In this chapter, we have explored Psalm 25:22, which at first glance appears as a plea from a people who have failed to obey God. We have learned that disobedience results in failure and deprives one of a position of favor, exchanging it for distress, anxiety, or danger. While God has made provisions for failure, the constant plea for redemption can express more the desire to do one's own will rather than the will of God. In the next chapter, "The Message of Oneness," we will delve into the importance of submitting our will to God and aligning our desires with His plan for our lives. We will learn how oneness with God can bring about blessings and fulfillment beyond what we can imagine.

Chapter 5

The Message of Oneness

John 5:19

To glorify God Is to be subjected to His Instructions, the root of which the greatest emphasis Is in the words: 'verily, verily your God Is one". The whole of this statement embraces a demonstration of the things we must do. Such instructions and demonstrations come through prayer; the action that intimately connects with our own life and destiny.

Oftentimes I have wondered whether Jesus remembers his "pre-earthly" state or whether he is in direct communication with God throughout his earthly ministry. This verse gives the answer, with the latter part revealing the constant and real intimacy shared between Jesus and the Father.

For Instance, the verse does not say what Jesus "has seen", but what he sees; the verb speaking in the present tense and as a continuing action. Thus, one concludes that as Jesus prays, he receives "foreknowledge" of what and how to do the things he must do. God gives us both instructions and illustrations as He did with Jesus, and so He does with those who diligently seek Him. It is in the seeking that one learns, 'He" is the source of all goodness, love, and power

Therefore, and as Jesus said to his disciples: 'Verily, verily, I say unto you, He that believeth on me, the works that I do shall he do also; and greater (works) than these shall he do; because I go unto the Father. John 14:12 KJV While Jesus was with the disciples, they were able to do exactly what Jesus did. However, when Jesus ascended, the ability of the "greater" began to reign and this affirmation was revealed on the day of Pentecost; the day when the Holy Spirit made his physical debut in the hearts and minds of men, with the "greater" being manifested, and demonstrated the complete harmony and unity in Heaven and Earth to propel evil.

Thus, we cannot minimize or take for granted the time spent with God. It is within these times we best understand concerns, situations, or problems. Likewise, it is during these times that 'greater' comes to us and we receive instruction or better still, o demonstration of what to do. These revelations are certain, situational, and given to an immediately appointed time Herein, is the mystery of the manifold variety of "creative activity" as given to the absolute promise that engages the Kingdom of God.

Even more, the process is similar to the need for daily bread. Oftentimes we may not know when or exactly what we will eat, but the result remains a supply for needs. As sure as we feel hunger, we will "eat" as God gives provisions for that day Likewise, as we go through the day, we may not know when we are given to be blessed but for certain, within every moment is an opportunity for the 'greater part of us' to operate in accordance with His instructions and demonstrations

Thus, the 'Message of Oneness' is manifested where one does not neglect prayer nor resist divine instruction, but rather yields to active demonstration and the overall mandate to glorify God in all that is oneness with Him.

Introduction: The Message of Oneness

In this chapter titled "The Message of Oneness," we explore John 5:19, which emphasizes the importance of glorifying God by submitting to His instructions. The statement "verily, verily your God is one" highlights the need for unity and oneness with God, which can be achieved through prayer and seeking divine instruction.

John 5:19 (KJV):

"Then answered Jesus and said unto them, Verily, verily, I say unto you, The Son can do nothing of himself, but what he seeth the Father do: for what things soever he doeth, these also doeth the Son likewise."

Original Text:

To glorify God Is to be subjected to His Instructions, the root of which the greatest emphasis Is in the words: 'verily, verily your God Is one". The whole of this statement embraces a demonstration of the things we must do. Such instructions and demonstrations come through prayer; the action that intimately connects with our own life and destiny.

Commentary:

This chapter explores the message of oneness as expressed in John 5:19 and the importance of being subject to God's instructions in order to glorify Him. The emphasis on the oneness of God underscores the need for unity in following His will. Instructions and demonstrations come through prayer, which is a means of connecting with God on a deep level and understanding our own life's purpose and destiny.

Reflective Question:

How can prayer help us understand God's instructions for our lives and connect with our purpose and destiny?

Original Text:

Oftentimes I have wondered whether Jesus remembers his "pre-earthly" state or whether he is in direct communication with God throughout his earthly ministry. This verse gives the answer, with the latter part revealing the constant and real intimacy shared between Jesus and the Father. For instance, the verse does not say what Jesus "has seen", but what he sees; the verb speaking in the present tense and as a continuing action. Thus, one concludes that as Jesus prays, he receives "fore-knowledge" of what and how to do the things he must do.

Commentary:

The verse in John 5:19 suggests that Jesus is in constant communication with God throughout his earthly ministry and receives "fore-knowledge" of what he must do through prayer. This emphasizes the importance of prayer in seeking guidance and understanding in our own lives.

Reflective Question:

In what ways can we develop a deeper connection with God through prayer and receive guidance and understanding in our lives?

Original Text:

God gives us both instructions and illustrations as He did with Jesus, and so He does with those who diligently seek Him. It is in the seeking that one learns, 'He" is the source of all goodness, love, and power. Therefore, as Jesus said to his disciples, "Verily, verily, I say unto you, He that believeth on me, the works that I do shall he do also; and greater (works) than these shall he do; because I go unto the Father" (John 14:12, KJV).

Commentary:

God provides instructions and illustrations to those who diligently seek Him, just as He did with Jesus. By seeking God through prayer and faith, we can learn that He is the source of all goodness, love, and power. Jesus promised that those who believe in Him would do even greater works than He did, emphasizing the power of faith and the connection with God.

Reflective Question:

How can we cultivate a stronger faith and connection with God to be able to do even greater works than Jesus did?

Original Text:

The ability of the "greater" began to reign after Jesus ascended, and this affirmation was revealed on the day of Pentecost, when the Holy Spirit made his physical debut in the hearts and minds of men. The "greater" being manifested demonstrated the complete harmony and unity in Heaven and Earth to propel evil. Thus, we cannot minimize or take for granted the time spent with God. It is within these times that we best understand concerns, situations, or problems. Likewise, it is during these times that the 'greater' comes to us, and we receive instruction or better still, a demonstration of what to do. These revelations are certain, situational, and given at an immediately appointed time. Herein lies the mystery of the manifold variety of "creative activity" as given to the absolute promise that engages the Kingdom of God.

Commentary:

The day of Pentecost marked a turning point in the ability of believers to do even greater works than Jesus did, as the Holy Spirit made a physical debut in the hearts and minds of men. This manifestation of the "greater" demonstrated the harmony and unity between Heaven and Earth that can overcome evil. The importance of spending time with God through prayer is emphasized, as it is during these times that we can understand our concerns, situations, or problems and receive guidance and instruction. These revelations are specific and timely, and they engage us in the creative activity of the Kingdom of God.

Reflective Question:

How can we recognize and respond to the revelations and guidance we receive from God during times of prayer and seeking Him? How can we engage in the creative activity of the Kingdom of God?

Conclusion: The Power of Oneness with God

Through John 5:19, we have learned about the importance of prayer and seeking a deeper connection with God to understand His instructions and fulfill our purpose in life. We have also seen how Jesus, through constant communication with God, was able to receive foreknowledge of what he must do. By seeking God with diligence, we can receive His instructions and demonstrations just as Jesus did.

The message of oneness emphasizes the unity and harmony we can achieve with God through prayer and faith. It is in these moments that we best understand our concerns, situations, and problems, and receive the "greater" that comes to us. This revelation is given at an appointed time, revealing the manifold variety of creative activity that comes from being one with God.

Chapter 6

Counsels of the Hearts and Praise of God

1 Corinthians 4:5

In September 1995, God revealed to me a guiding principle that has remained with me since that time. The principle is that what appears is not what it is; a profound acknowledgment, suggestive of perceptive limitations in experience or engagements of the ordinary and the extraordinary. This is the conclusion that more is happening with us, in us, around us, and to us than we can completely comprehend or conceptualize.

To judge is to give pre-notion to a presentation rather than the total representation. The single (but most applied) ability to judge or lend thought and interpretation of one's surroundings underscores the limitation of the human ability to accurately assess or understand the phenomenon.

Man's senses are limited in dimensions; up and down, in and out, front and back, left and right. The creation, however, is multi-dimensional and its' sphere embraces diagonal circumferences and the invisible. It is the limitations of humanness that veils complete reality from the senses; a single sense, intuition, being underutilized and left in obscurity.

Until the Lord comes, there is only presumption, supposition, and judicial rule; the product being finite rather than infinite in scope. He alone has the capacity to bring to light the hidden things of darkness, the counsels of the hearts, and the inspiration of man's praise of God.

Where total reality becomes ultimate truth, revealed will be the essence of all things, and then every man shall praise and have praise of God; a oneness that beckons the soul into eternity.

Introduction: Counsels of Heart and Praise

The ability to judge and interpret our surroundings is a fundamental aspect of human experience. However, as revealed in 1 Corinthians 4:5, the limitations of the human ability to accurately assess or understand the phenomenon underscores the profound acknowledgment that what appears is not what it is. There is more happening with us, in us, around us, and to us than we have the ability to completely comprehend or conceptualize. This realization highlights the limitations of humanness in perceiving reality and underscores the importance of relying on the Lord for guidance.

Man's senses are limited in dimensions, which veil complete reality from the senses. However, creation is multi-dimensional and embraces diagonal circumferences and the invisible, suggesting that there is more to reality than meets the eye. It is only through the Lord's revelation that we can uncover the hidden things of darkness, the counsels of the hearts, and the inspiration of man's praise of God.

This chapter explores the limitations of human perception and the importance of relying on the Lord for guidance. It emphasizes the importance of humility in judgment and the necessity of recognizing that our perceptions may be incomplete or flawed. Ultimately, the chapter underscores the importance of praising God and seeking his guidance in all aspects of life.

1 Corinthians 4:5:

Therefore, judge nothing before the time, until the Lord come, who both will bring to light the hidden things of darkness and will make manifest the counsels of the hearts: and then shall every man have praise of God.

Original Text:

In September 1995, God revealed to me a guiding principle that has remained with me since that time. The principle is that what appears is not what it is; a profound acknowledgment, suggestive of perceptive limitations in experience or engagements of the ordinary and the extraordinary. This is the conclusion that more is happening with us, in us, around us, and to us than we have the ability to completely comprehend or conceptualize.

Commentary:

The statement highlights a profound insight into the nature of reality and human perception. The idea that what appears is not necessarily what it is suggests that our perception is limited and that there may be more going on around us than we can comprehend. This insight is particularly important in the context of spirituality, as it suggests that there may be spiritual dimensions to reality that are not immediately apparent.

The acknowledgment of perceptive limitations in experience and engagement with the ordinary and extraordinary suggests that our understanding of reality is limited by our experiences and perceptions. Our experiences are limited by our senses and the interpretations we make based on them. This limitation means that we can only perceive a small portion of reality, which is filtered through our senses and our interpretations of them.

The idea that there may be more happening with us, in us, around us, and to us than we can comprehend or conceptualize is a humbling realization that highlights our limitations as human beings. It suggests that there may be spiritual dimensions to reality that are beyond our comprehension and that we must remain open to the possibility of the extraordinary.

Reflective Question:

How can the acknowledgment of our perceptive limitations and the possibility of spiritual dimensions to reality help us in our spiritual journey? How can we remain open to the possibility of the extraordinary in our daily lives?

Original Text:

To judge is to give pre-notion to a presentation rather than the total representation. The single (but most applied) ability to judge or lend thought and interpretation of one's surroundings underscores the limitation of the human ability to accurately assess or understand the phenomenon.

Commentary:

This statement highlights the limitation of the human ability to accurately assess or understand a phenomenon. To judge something or someone is to form a preconceived notion based on a limited representation or understanding of the situation or person. This preconceived notion can lead to misunderstandings and misinterpretations of the reality of the situation. It is important to recognize that our ability to judge is limited by our personal biases, experiences, and understanding of the world.

In many cases, we judge others based on their outward appearances, actions, or words without considering the underlying circumstances or motivations behind their behavior. This can result in negative attitudes, prejudices, and discrimination.

Instead of judging others based on limited representations, it is important to seek understanding and empathy toward others. We should try to approach situations with an open mind and a willingness to listen and learn. This will help us to gain a more accurate understanding of the situation and the motivations behind the actions of others.

Original Text:

Man's senses are limited in dimensions; up and down, in and out, front and back, left and right. The creation, however, is multi-dimensional and its' sphere embraces diagonal circumferences and the invisible. It is the limitations of humanness that veils complete reality from the senses; a single sense, intuition, being underutilized and left in obscurity.

Reflective Question:

Have you ever judged someone based on a limited representation or understanding of the situation? How can you cultivate a mindset of empathy and understanding towards others to overcome these limitations and approach situations with an open mind?

Commentary:

This statement highlights the inherent limitations of human perception and the ability to fully comprehend the complexity of the world we live in. The human senses are limited to certain dimensions, namely up and down, in and out, front and back, left and right. However, the world we live in is multi-dimensional, embracing diagonal circumferences and the invisible. This means that there is much that exists beyond our perceptual limitations, and our understanding of reality is necessarily limited by our human experience.

The statement also notes that intuition, which is the ability to understand something instinctively, is often underutilized and left in obscurity. This suggests that relying solely on the five senses to make sense of the world around us is not enough and that there may be an innate wisdom that we are not tapping into. Perhaps by acknowledging and tapping into our intuition, we can expand our understanding of the world beyond what is immediately perceptible.

Reflective Question:

In what ways have you experienced the limitations of human perception in your own life, and how have you tried to expand your understanding of the world beyond what is immediately perceptible? Have you ever relied on your intuition to guide your understanding of a situation and if so, what did it manifest?

Original Text:

Until the Lord comes, there is only presumption, supposition, and judicial rule; the product being finite rather than infinite in scope. He alone has the capacity to bring to light the hidden things of darkness, the counsels of the hearts, and the inspiration of man's praise of God.

Commentary:

The statement "Until the Lord comes, there is only presumption, supposition, and judicial rule" underscores the limitation of human understanding and points to the need for divine intervention to shed light on the mysteries of life. Despite our best efforts, our ability to grasp the essence of things remains finite, and our judgments often fall short of the mark. This is because our perception is constrained by our finite nature, and we cannot see beyond what our senses allow us to see.

The statement goes on to affirm that only God has the capacity to reveal the hidden things of darkness, the counsels of the hearts, and the inspiration of man's praise of God. This points to the fact that there is a deeper reality that exists beyond what we can see or comprehend. The unseen world is as real as the world we perceive with our senses, and it is only through divine revelation that we can begin to fathom its mysteries.

The statement suggests that when the Lord comes, he will bring to light the hidden things of darkness, the counsels of the hearts, and the inspiration of man's praise of God. This implies that there is a time when all truth will be revealed, and every knee will bow and confess that Jesus Christ is Lord. This is a comforting thought for believers who may feel over-whelmed by the mysteries of life and the limited understand-ing of the world we possess.

Reflective Question:

How does the belief in God's capacity to reveal the hidden things of darkness, the counsels of the hearts, and the inspi-ration of man's praise of God impact your understanding of the world?

Original Text:

Where total reality becomes ultimate truth, revealed will be the essence of all things, and then every man shall praise and have praise of God; a oneness that beckons the soul into eternity.

Commentary:

This statement emphasizes the idea that there is more to reality than what is visible to the human senses. It suggests there is a deeper truth to existence that is beyond human comprehension. It is only when this ultimate truth is revealed that all things will be fully understood, and every person will be able to praise and have praise of God. This idea can be re-lated to the concept of transcendence, which is a higher reality beyond the physical world that can only be perceived through intuition or spiritual experience.

This statement also highlights the importance of praising God. It suggests that praising God is not just a religious ritual but a way to connect with the ultimate truth and experience a sense of oneness with the divine. It is through praise that one can transcend the limitations of human perception and gain a glimpse of the ultimate reality.

Reflective Question:

How does the idea of ultimate truth and transcendence impact your perception of reality and your relationship with God?

Conclusion: Counsels of the Hearts and Praise of God

The collection of texts explored in this chapter highlights the limitations of human perception and the importance of seeking divine guidance to gain a deeper understanding of reality. Underscored is the idea that our ability to judge and interpret our surroundings is limited and that there is much more happening with us, in us, around us, and to us than we can fully comprehend or conceptualize. The chapter emphasizes the importance of humility in judgment, the necessity of recognizing our limitations, and the importance of seeking guidance from the Lord.

The texts also highlight the importance of praising God, both as a way to connect with the ultimate truth and to gain a deeper understanding of reality. The idea that total reality becomes ultimate truth and that every man shall praise and have praise of God, suggests that there is a higher reality beyond what we can perceive with our senses. It is only when this ultimate truth is revealed that all things will be fully understood, and every person will be able to connect with the divine and experience a sense of oneness with the ultimate reality.

Chapter 7

Ransom, Redemption, Repentance, and Restoration

Hosea 13:14

A complete reading of Hosea Chapter 13 finds Israel in "a" height of forgetfulness, dishonor, and blatant sin, and God admonishes them, through the Prophet Hosea, with details of His impending wrath because of their sin.

This verse, embedded and subtle, speaks to hope, in spite of the certain destruction to come; God's ultimate mercy breaking forth from the depths of His unfailing love and compassion. Although they sin more and more, God acknowledges they have done this according to their own understanding; suggesting that sin "more and more" is the result of an understanding not given by God. What a generation passes to the next generation must be godly, or else that fruit is and exists in corruption.

God's word, however, is timeless and exists through eternity. When given to the ultimate state of man's tendency to sin, God holds dear everyone created. Like gold coming forth from a fiery furnace, so too will be the souls of those who failed to reconcile repentance when presented. Even so, God's promise is He will ransom them from the power of the grave and redeem them from death; a death where repentance has no role, grace overshadows justice, and mercy pleads restoration. Thus, the things that are impossible for men are possible with God. Luke 18:27.

Introduction: Ransom, Redemption, Repentance, and Restoration

In this chapter, we will explore the powerful message of Hosea 13:14, which speaks to the themes of ransom, redemption, repentance, and restoration. The verse is embedded within a larger context of admonishment for Israel's forgetfulness, dishonor, sin, and the impending wrath of God. However, amidst this dark backdrop, we find a glimmer of hope and God's ultimate mercy breaking forth from the depths of His unfailing love and compassion. Through this verse, we will delve into the timeless nature of God's word and the promise of redemption and restoration, even for those who have sinned and strayed from His path. We will also examine the importance of repentance and the power of grace and mercy in the face of justice.

Hosea 13:14:

"I will ransom them from the power of the grave; I will redeem them from death: O death, I will be thy plagues; O grave, I will be thy destruction: repentance shall be hidden from mine eyes."

Original Text:

A complete reading of Hosea Chapter 13 finds Israel in a height of forgetfulness, dishonor, and blatant sin, and God admonishes them, through the Prophet Hosea, with details of His impending wrath because of their sin.

Commentary:

This paragraph highlights the context of Hosea 13 and sets the tone for the chapter. The prophet Hosea's message to Israel is one of admonishment and warning of God's impending wrath. Israel is depicted as being in a state of forgetfulness, dishonor, and blatant sin, having turned away from God's ways. The emphasis on God's wrath and judgment underscores the seriousness of Israel's sin and the urgency for repentance. This paragraph sets the stage for the exploration of ransom, redemption, repentance, and restoration; highlighting the need for God's mercy and grace in the face of sin.

Reflective Question:

How does the message in Hosea Chapter 13 apply to our own lives, and what can we learn from God's admonishment of Israel's sin?

Original Text:

This verse, embedded and subtle, speaks to hope, in spite of the certain destruction to come; God's ultimate mercy breaking forth from the depths of His unfailing love and compassion. Although they sin more and more, God acknowledges they have done this according to their own understanding; suggesting that sin "more and more" is the result of an understanding not given by God. What a generation passes to the next generation must be godly, or else that fruit is and exists in corruption.

Commentary:

Despite Israel's blatant sin and impending destruction, Hosea 13:14 provides a glimmer of hope with the promise of God's ultimate mercy breaking forth from His unfailing love and compassion. The verse suggests that sinning "more and more" is the result of an understanding not given by God, emphasizing the importance of passing down godly teachings from one generation to the next. It highlights the role of personal responsibility in understanding God's will and living a righteous life.

Reflective Question:

How can we ensure that we are passing down godly teachings to the next generation and living a life in accordance with God's will?

Original Text:

God's word, however, is timeless and exists through eternity. When given to the ultimate state of man's tendency to sin, God holds dear everyone created. Like gold coming forth from a fiery furnace, so too will be the souls of those who failed to reconcile repentance when presented. Even so, God's promise is He will ransom them from the power of the grave and redeem them from death; a death where repentance has no role, grace overshadows justice, and mercy pleads restoration. Thus, the things that are impossible for men are possible with God. Luke 18:27

Commentary:

The final paragraph of this chapter reflects on the timelessness and enduring nature of God's word. Despite humanity's tendency towards sin, God values each and every person He created. The imagery of gold coming forth from a fiery furnace suggests that even those who fail to reconcile and repent in this life still have hope for redemption in the next. This message of hope is reinforced by the inclusion of Luke 18:27, which reminds us that the things that seem impossible for us are possible with God.

It is worth noting that this chapter draws from several different passages of the Bible to convey its message. This highlights the importance of studying and examining the fullness of God's word, rather than simply focusing on isolated verses or passages. By exploring the full breadth of scripture, we can gain a more comprehensive understanding of God's message and plan for our lives.

Reflective Question:

How does God's promise to ransom and redeem us give us hope in the face of our own shortcomings and sinfulness?

Conclusion: Ransom, Redemption, Repentance, and Restoration

Hosea 13:14 speaks to the themes of ransom, redemption, repentance, and restoration, even in the face of Israel's forgetfulness, dishonor, and sin. The promise of God's ultimate mercy breaking forth from His unfailing love and compassion provides a glimmer of hope amidst the darkness of impending destruction. This chapter has explored the timeless nature of God's word and the importance of repentance, grace, and mercy in the face of justice. It also highlights the need to pass down godly teachings to future generations and the value of studying the fullness of God's word. In the next chapter, "Understanding the Animate and Inanimate," we will delve into the distinction between animate and inanimate objects and how this understanding can inform our relationship with God and the world around us.

Chapter 8

Understanding the Animate and Inanimate

1 Thessalonians 4:8

To despise is to dislike something intensely and with contempt, which is to hate; an emotion rooted in the subconscious. When distinguishing the animate from the inanimate, there needs to be proper placement of emotions through man's senses. God has provisioned man, and developed senses: to see, smell, hear, feel, taste, and intuition; 'developed' because they are consciously and subconsciously manifested. However, and while intuition is underused and thereby least developed from among the other senses, hate is not listed. For man cannot hate himself, only inanimate things. Hate, therefore, functions within intuition but is often misplaced in the application.

Jesus taught his disciples, no man can serve two masters; for either he will hate the one and love the other, or else he will hold to the one and despise the other, Matthew 6:24. Ye cannot serve God (animate) and mammon (inanimate). Mammon is the personification of wealth as a god and when sought or hoarded, begets evil and corrupt influence. In that, no man hates or can hate that which is like him/herself, hate then, has its root in an inanimate thing not readily manifested but subjected to intuition.

Intuition is man's 'golden cord' to God and its use aligns the senses toward proper application and intuition alerts us to the good and bad of existence; stimulating the other senses and in turn, eliciting an action response. Man, however, tends to subordinate the intuition barometer; this resulting in improper placement of intense emotions and a false read on the senses.

Thus, it is not a person that is despised but rather, the absence of the Holy Spirit in the proper comprehension of a "thing" as animate or inanimate.

Introduction: Understanding the Animate and Inanimate

The concept of hate is a complex and often misunderstood emotion, especially when it comes to distinguishing between animate and inanimate objects. In this chapter, we will explore the teachings of Jesus in Matthew 6:24 and the importance of properly placing emotions through man's senses. We will examine the role of intuition, the least developed of our senses, and its crucial role in aligning our senses toward proper application. Through the lens of 1 Thessalonians 4:8, we will learn about the danger of hate and how it is often misplaced due to improper use of our senses. Ultimately, we will discover that proper understanding of the animate and inanimate comes from an alignment with the Holy Spirit, leading to a deeper comprehension of the world around us.

1 Thessalonians 4:8:

"He therefore that despiseth, despiseth not man, but God, who hath also given unto us his Holy Spirit."

Original Text:

To despise is to dislike something intensely and with contempt, which is to hate; an emotion rooted in the subconscious. When distinguishing the animate from the inanimate, there needs to be proper placement of emotions through man's senses. God has provisioned man, and developed senses; to see, smell, hear, feel, taste, and intuition; 'developed' because they are consciously and subconsciously manifested. However, and while intuition is underused and thereby least developed, from among the other senses note that hate is not listed. For man cannot hate himself, only inanimate things. Hate, therefore, functions within intuition but is often misplaced in application.

Commentary:

This paragraph explores the concept of hate and how it is rooted in the subconscious. The author notes that hate is often misplaced in the application, particularly when distinguishing between the animate and inanimate. While God has provided man with senses to perceive and interpret the world around us, intuition is underused and least developed. The author points out that hate is not listed among the other senses, suggesting that it is a function of intuition. This misplaced emotion can lead to improper placement of intense emotions and a false interpretation of the world around us.

Reflective Question:

How can we ensure that we properly place our emotions and interpret the world around us, particularly when distinguishing between the animate and inanimate?

Original Text:

Jesus taught his disciples, no man can serve two masters; for either he will hate the one and love the other, or else he will hold to the one and despise the other, Matthew 6:24. Ye cannot serve God (animate) and mammon (inanimate). Mammon is the personification of wealth as a god and when sought or hoarded, begets evil and corrupt influence. In that, no man hates or can hate that which is like him/herself, hate then, has its root in an inanimate thing not readily manifested but subjected to intuition.

Commentary:

The passage from Matthew 6:24 underscores the importance of the proper placement of emotions and devotion to God. Jesus warns against serving two masters, as it will result in a divided heart and misplaced emotions. Mammon, the personification of wealth as a god, is an example of an inanimate thing that can be mistakenly placed above God in our devotion and desire. Hate, as discussed in the previous paragraph, can have its root in an inanimate thing, such as wealth, that is not readily manifested but is subjected to intuition.

Reflective Question:

How can we ensure that our devotion and emotions are properly placed and aligned with God's will, and not inanimate things like wealth or material possessions?

Original Text:

Intuition is man's 'golden cord' to God and its use aligns the senses toward proper application, intuition alerts us to the good and bad of existence; stimulating the other senses and in turn, eliciting an action response. Man, however, tends to subordinate the intuition barometer, this resulting in improper placement of intense emotions and a false read on the senses.

Commentary:

This paragraph emphasizes the importance of intuition as a crucial aspect of the human senses and its role in aligning us with God's will. It highlights how intuition serves as a "golden cord" that connects us to God and alerts us to the good and bad of existence, eliciting an action response. However, it notes that man often subordinates this intuition barometer, leading to the improper placement of intense emotions and a false interpretation of our senses.

Reflective Question:

In what ways have you experienced the influence of intuition in your life, and how have you responded to it? How can you develop a better understanding of your intuition and use it to align yourself with God's will?

Original Text:

Thus, it is not a person that is despised but rather, the absence of the Holy Spirit in the proper comprehension of a "thing" as animate or inanimate.

Commentary:

The chapter concludes with a strong emphasis on the importance of properly comprehending the animate and inanimates to avoid feelings of hatred and contempt. It is suggested that when we experience these emotions, it is not actually the object of our hatred that we despise, but rather our own misunderstanding or lack of discernment regarding its true nature. This lack of understanding is attributed to the absence of the Holy Spirit in our lives. Therefore, we are encouraged to rely more on our intuition, which is described as our "golden cord" to God that properly aligns our senses and emotions toward good and truth.

Reflective Question:

How can we rely more on our intuition and the guidance of the Holy Spirit to properly discern and comprehend the animate and inanimate in our lives, and avoid misplaced emotions such as hate and contempt?

Conclusion: Understanding the Animate and Inanimate

In this chapter, we have explored the importance of the proper placement of emotions through man's senses when distinguishing between the animate and inanimate. We have seen how hate, a powerful emotion rooted in the subconscious, can often be misplaced in its application, leading to improper placement of intense emotions and a false read on the senses. We have also learned how intuition, man's 'golden cord' to God, plays a crucial role in aligning our senses towards proper application and alerting us to the good and bad of existence.

Through Jesus' teachings, we have been reminded of the danger of serving two masters and the corrupting influence of mammon, the personification of wealth as a god. We have seen how hate, rooted in an inanimate thing and not readily manifested, can have its root in intuition, but when subjected to the Holy Spirit's guidance, can be rightly placed.

In the next chapter, "Correction with Judgment, Not Anger," we will explore the biblical perspective on correction and judgment. We will delve into the difference between righteous judgment and anger and how God's corrective measures are motivated by love and mercy, rather than anger or punishment. We will also examine the role of forgiveness and restoration in correction, and how we can apply these principles in our daily lives.

Chapter 9

Correction with Judgment, Not Anger

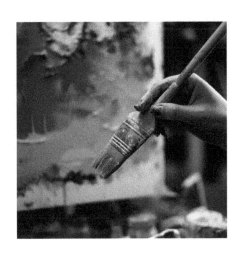

Jeremiah 10:24

Correct me Lord but with your word, rather than your anger, wherein is my own hurt, and cause for me to perish.

In the words of Matthew Henry:

He deprecates the divine wrath, that it might not fall upon God's Israel. He speaks not for himself only, but on the behalf of this people: 0 Lord correct me, but with judgment (in measure and with moderation, and in wisdom, no more than is necessary for driving out the foolishness that is bound up in our hearts: not in thy anger (how severe so ever the correction be, let it come from thy love, and be designed for our good and made to work for good), not to bring us to nothing, but to bring us home to thyself. Let it not be according to the desert of our sins, but according to the design of thy grace. We cannot pray in faith that we may never be corrected, while we are conscious to ourselves that we need correction and deserve it and know that as much as God loves he chastens. The great thing we should dread in affliction is the wrath of God. Say not, Lord, do not correct me, but, Lord, do not correct me in anger; for that will infuse wormwood and gall into the affliction and misery that will bring us to nothing. We may bear the smart of his rod. but we cannot bear the weight of his wrath. (Matthew Henry's Complete Commentary on the Bible, Studylight.org)

Mr. Henry had the right idea and was quite on point regarding the ultimate end of those who kindle the anger of the Lord. Deuteronomy 6:16 states: do what he commands (for the Lord thy God (is) a jealous God among you), lest the anger of the Lord thy God be kindled against thee and destroy thee from off the face of the earth.

It is good that God is slow to anger. However, it is His anger rather than his love that too much emphasis is given. The Bible speaks of the enduring love of God, but the blatant sin and acts of sin stir His most anxious and desirable patience.

Those whom He loves, He chastens, but unto those who provoke Him to anger with the works of their hands, they do so to their own hurt and to whom He will destroy from the face of the earth.

Introduction: Correction with Judgement, Not Anger

The chapter "Correction with Judgment, Not Anger" emphasizes the importance of seeking correction from the Lord through His Word rather than anger, drawing inspiration from Jeremiah 10:24 and the **Commentary** of theologian Matthew Henry, who stressed the need for wisdom and moderation in correction. The author highlights that God's enduring love is often overshadowed by an overemphasis on His anger, and concludes with a warning from Deuteronomy 6:16 to obey God's commands and avoid provoking His anger.

Jeremiah 10:24:

"O Lord, correct me, but with judgment; not in thine anger, lest thou bring me to nothing."

Original Text:

Mr. Henry had the right idea and was quite on point regarding the ultimate end of those who kindle the anger of the Lord. Deuteronomy 6:16 states do what he commands (for the Lord thy God (is) a jealous God among you), lest the anger of the Lord thy God be kindled against thee and destroy thee from off the face of the earth.

Commentary:

The **Commentary** highlights the importance of obedience to God's commands and avoiding behaviors that provoke His anger. The author refers to Deuteronomy 6:16 as a warning that disobedience can lead to destruction. This verse emphasizes the holiness of God and the need for reverence and respect in our relationship with Him.

Reflective Question:

How can we cultivate a deeper understanding and respect for God's holiness and avoid behaviors that provoke His anger?

Original Text:

It is good that God is slow to anger. However, it is His anger rather than his love that too much emphasis is given. The Bible speaks of the enduring love of God, but the blatant sin and acts of sin stir His most anxious and desirable patience.

Commentary:

The author in this statement is highlighting the common tendency to focus more on God's anger than on His love, despite the Bible's emphasis on God's enduring love for His people. The author acknowledges that God is slow to anger, but also notes that sin and disobedience can provoke His anger. The author encourages readers to focus more on God's love and strive to live in obedience to His commands.

Reflective Question:
How can we balance our understanding of God's love and His anger in our lives and in our relationships with others?

Original Text:
Those whom He loves, He chastens, but unto those who provoke Him to anger with the works of their hands, they do so to their own hurt and to whom He will destroy from the face of the earth.

Commentary:
This statement reflects the biblical principle that God corrects and disciplines those whom He loves, in order to help them grow and mature. However, for those who persist in rebellion and disobedience, they will ultimately face judgment and destruction. It highlights the importance of acknowledging God's sovereignty and seeking to obey His commands, rather than provoking His anger through sinful behavior.

Reflective Question:
How can we distinguish between the loving correction and discipline of God and the destructive consequences of our own disobedience and rebellion?

Conclusion: Correction with Judgement, Not Anger

The chapter highlights the importance of seeking correction from God through His Word while avoiding His anger. The emphasis is on wisdom and moderation in correction, and on striving to live in obedience to God's commands, rather than provoking His anger through sin and disobedience. As we seek to understand God's holiness and balance our understanding of His love and anger, we are challenged to examine our own lives and behaviors and to cultivate a deeper reverence and respect for God's sovereignty. By doing so, we can grow in our faith and avoid the destructive consequences of rebellion and disobedience.

Chapter 10

The Healing Balm of Righteousness

Revelation 22:14

It is not enough to know God's commandments; blessed are they that do His commandments. For unto these will be the winning of souls and healing for many.

To be blessed is the bringing of happiness and/or good fortune. It is a word expressed in the past, its' direction, however, forward and continuing. The idea is one of acknowledgment of one's obedience to God and because of obedience, there is an immediate, present, and future bestowing of considerable favor from God, through the blessed, to those needing to be blessed.

And the scripture was fulfilled which saith, Abraham believed God, and it was imputed unto him for righteousness; and he was called the Friend of God (Jm. 2:23). To believe God is to obey God. Obedience makes us a friend of God and as a friend, we are stewards of a great nation: the Kingdom of God.

The two uses of the word "may" in the above scripture sets the tone and creates synergy for activity engaged by the blessed; the activity, the tree as given to but forsaken by Adam and Eve, remains a choice yet fulfilled by the blessed. It is this activity, this tree, this lifestyle wherein hangs the leaves of twelve fruits (Rev. 22:2) of righteousness: love, joy, peace, caring, longsuffering, gentleness, obedience, faith, meekness, temperance, goodness, and mercy; the tree given to the blessed for the benefit of humanity.

For the fruit of the righteous, the blessed, friends of God is a tree of life; a wise lifestyle that wins souls monthly (Prov 11:30 AEL-W paraphrased), and has access into the city for the healing of the nations (Rev. 22.2), or the people in a land (the Kingdom of God) under God's governance.

Therefore, they that are blessed are those heeding the first and greatest commandment; this heeding, in turn, bestows to them righteous living, and this lifestyle wins souls and is the healing balm for many.

Introduction: The Healing Balm of Righteousness

The chapter titled "The Healing Balm of Righteousness" emphasizes the importance of not only knowing God's commandments but also obeying them. Drawing inspiration from Revelation 22:14, the author notes that it is not enough to simply know God's commandments, but rather those who do His commandments will be blessed and able to win souls and bring healing to many. The chapter discusses the meaning of being blessed and the role obedience plays in becoming a friend of God and a steward of His kingdom. The chapter also highlights the importance of a righteous lifestyle, which is characterized by the twelve fruits of righteousness and has the power to win souls and bring healing to nations.

Revelation 22:14:

"Blessed are they that do his commandments, that they may have right to the tree of life, and may enter in through the gates into the city."

Original Text:

It is not enough to know God's commandments; blessed are they that do His commandments. For unto these will be the winning of souls and healing for many.

Commentary:

This statement emphasizes the importance of putting God's commandments into practice, rather than simply knowing them. The author suggests that those who obey God's commandments are blessed, and that their obedience leads to the winning of souls and the healing of many. This highlights the practical nature of faith and the importance of living out one's beliefs in a way that positively impacts others.

Reflective Question:

How can we actively seek to put God's commandments into practice in our daily lives, and what impact can our obedience have on the people around us?

Original Text:

To be blessed is the bringing of happiness and/or good fortune. It is a word expressed in the past, its' direction, however forward and continuing. The idea is one of acknowledgment of one's obedience to God and because of obedience, there is an immediate, present, and future bestowing of considerable favor from God, through the blessed, to those needing to be blessed.

Commentary:

In this statement, the author defines the concept of being "blessed" and highlights its significance in the context of obedience to God's commandments. The author notes that being blessed involves not just past experiences of happiness or good fortune, but also present and future blessings that stem from obedience to God. The author suggests that being blessed is a result of acknowledging one's obedience to God and fulfilling His commandments, which leads to considerable favor from God that can be shared with others in need of blessings.

Reflective Question:
How can we cultivate a deeper understanding of what it means to be "blessed" and how can we share our blessings with those in need around us?

Original Text:
And the scripture was fulfilled which saith, Abraham believed God, and it was imputed unto him for righteousness; and he was called the Friend of God (Jm. 2:23). To believe God is to obey God. Obedience makes us a friend of God and as a friend, we are stewards of a great nation; the Kingdom of God.

Commentary:
This statement highlights the intimate relationship between belief in God and obedience to His commands. The example of Abraham, who believed God and was considered righteous, emphasizes the importance of faith in action. The idea that obedience makes us a friend of God underscores the idea that our relationship with God is not just about following rules, but about cultivating a deep and meaningful connection with Him. As stewards of the Kingdom of God, we have a responsibility to live out our faith and share it with others.

Reflective Question:
How can we deepen our relationship with God through obedience and become better stewards of His kingdom?

Original Text:
The two uses of the word "may" in the above scripture set the tone and creates synergy for activity engaged by the blessed;

the activity, the tree as given to but forsaken by Adam and Eve, remains a choice yet fulfilled by the blessed. It is this activity, this tree, this lifestyle wherein hangs the leaves of twelve fruits (Rev. 22:2) of righteousness; love, joy, peace, caring, longsuffering, gentleness, obedience, faith, meekness, temperance, goodness, and mercy; the tree given to the blessed for the benefit of humanity.

Commentary:

In the preceding scripture, the word "may" is used twice, setting the tone and creating a synergy of activity for the blessed. The activity, symbolized by the tree given to Adam and Eve but subsequently forsaken, is now a choice that is fulfilled by the blessed. This choice involves a lifestyle that produces the twelve fruits of righteousness, including love, joy, peace, caring, longsuffering, gentleness, obedience, faith, meekness, temperance, goodness, and mercy, which are represented by the leaves on the tree of life (Rev. 22:2). The use of "may" indicates that the decision to engage in this activity is left to the individual. It is not forced upon them, but rather, it is a choice that they can make. Ultimately, this lifestyle benefits not only the blessed but also humanity as a whole.

Reflective Question:

How can we make the choice to engage in the activity of living a righteous lifestyle that produces fruit and benefits humanity?

Original Text:

For the fruit of the righteous, the blessed, friends of God is a tree of life; a wise lifestyle that wins souls monthly (Prov 11:30 AEL-W paraphrased), and has access into the city for the healing of the nations (Rev. 22.2), or the people in a land (the kingdom of God) under God's governance.

Commentary:

The idea presented in this passage is that the righteous and blessed are like a tree of life, providing wisdom and guidance that can lead to the winning of souls and the healing of nations. This suggests that the righteous are not just individuals who follow God's commandments, but also ones who use their wisdom and good deeds to make a positive impact on the world around them. By following a wise lifestyle, they can serve as an example to others and create a ripple effect of positive change.

Reflective Question:

How can we use our actions and wisdom to create positive change in the world around us and lead others to a more righteous and blessed life?

Original Text:

Therefore, they that are blessed are those heeding the first and greatest commandment; this heeding, in turn, bestows to them righteous living, and this lifestyle wins souls and is the healing balm for many.

Commentary:

The statement highlights the importance of obedience to the first and greatest commandment of loving God with all our heart, soul, mind, and strength. This kind of obedience leads to a lifestyle of righteousness and enables us to become a blessing to others, particularly by sharing the good news of God's love and grace with those around us. The healing balm that this kind of righteous living brings is not only physical but also spiritual, as it helps to bring wholeness and restoration to broken lives and relationships.

Reflective Question:

How can we prioritize our relationship with God and cultivate a lifestyle of obedience that reflects our love for Him and
leads to a positive impact on the lives of those around us?

Conclusion: The Healing Balm of Righteousness

In conclusion, this chapter emphasizes the importance of living a righteous lifestyle that stems from obedience to God's commandments. This lifestyle is a choice that each individual must make and is characterized by the twelve fruits of righteousness that are represented by the leaves on the tree of life. The idea of being blessed involves acknowledging one's obedience to God, which leads to the bestowing of considerable favor from God upon the blessed. The chapter highlights the importance of faith in action, as exemplified by Abraham, who believed God and was considered righteous. The righteous lifestyle is a wise one that not only benefits the blessed but also those around them, as it can lead to the winning of souls and the healing of nations.

Chapter 11

Favor of the Lord

Proverbs 8:35

This proverb addresses the full nature of Wisdom, and it is in its entire reading that one finds the pathway to the practical aspects of life; this verse also answers the question of how to obtain the favor of the Lord.

It is noteworthy to understand there is no hidden wisdom, but to obtain Wisdom requires an inward searching that reveals clean hands and a pure heart. These qualities hasten Wisdom's application, such application being for the good of self and others. Thus, there is the requirement for one to study, observe, notice, or experience something necessary or personal for the process of wisdom to occur.

Wisdom as a noun is a companion to those who will have her. The application of wisdom as a verb, however, is more than the ability to make a decision. The ability to make decisions is inherent in everyone. Many reasoning processes, however, are forward and while the results of application may appear advantageous, favor is a distinguishable flavor (unique characteristic) of a believer.

Wisdom, then, precedes the appropriate extrinsic or intrinsic application of knowledge (clean hands) to a situation, to manifest one's motive (pure heart). For the believer, Wisdom's presence is a constant companion to those becoming more self-aware of God's delight and Wisdom's rejoicing; her pleasure being with the decisions or actions of the sons of men.

As she was from the beginning, so Wisdom is with the believer before an application; her presence glorifies God and assures favor of the Lord for those who listen to her, watch for her, lean on her, and apply her guidance.

Introduction: Favor of the Lord

This chapter delves into the nature of Wisdom and how it can lead to obtaining God's favor. Drawing inspiration from Proverbs 8:35, the author notes that Wisdom is not something that can be obtained through a superficial search, but rather requires an inward searching that reveals clean hands and a pure heart. The chapter discusses the difference between having wisdom as a noun and applying it as a verb, highlighting the importance of wisdom in decision-making for believers. The chapter also emphasizes the constant presence of Wisdom as a companion to the believer, guiding them in their actions and decisions towards pleasing God and obtaining His favor. Overall, this chapter invites readers to cultivate a deeper understanding of Wisdom and how it can lead to a life of favor in the eyes of the Lord.

Proverbs 8:35:

"For whoso findeth me findeth life, and shall obtain Favour of the Lord."

Original Text:

This proverb addresses the full nature of Wisdom, and it is in its entire reading that one finds the pathway to the practical aspects of life; this verse also answers the question of how to obtain the favor of the Lord.

Commentary:

The author emphasizes the importance of fully understanding the nature of Wisdom in order to find the pathway to practical aspects of life. This suggests that Wisdom is not just an abstract concept, but a practical guide that can be applied to everyday situations. The verse also addresses how to obtain the favor of the Lord, which suggests that Wisdom is not just a personal benefit, but something that can lead to a deeper connection with God. By understanding the full nature of Wisdom, we can obtain God's favor and apply her guidance in our daily lives.

Reflective Question:

How can we deepen our understanding of the nature of Wisdom and apply her guidance to obtain God's favor in our daily lives?

Original Text:

It is noteworthy to understand there is no hidden wisdom, but to obtain Wisdom requires an inward searching that reveals clean hands and a pure heart. These qualities hasten Wisdom's application, such application being for the good of self and others. Thus, there is the requirement for one to study, observe, notice, or experience something necessary or personal for the process of wisdom to occur.

Commentary:

The importance of actively seeking wisdom and the process of gaining it through inward searching is emphasized in this statement. To obtain wisdom, one must have clean hands and a pure heart, meaning a morally upright life free from deceit and wrongdoing, with genuine intentions and uncorrupted motives. These qualities are essential for the application of wisdom, which ultimately benefits both oneself and others. Therefore, gaining wisdom requires personal investment in studying, observing, noticing, or experiencing something necessary or relevant to the individual. By doing so, one can develop a deeper understanding and application of wisdom for the good of oneself and others.

Reflective Question:

What steps can we take to engage in inward searching and cultivate the qualities of clean hands and a pure heart in order to obtain wisdom and apply it for the benefit of ourselves and others?

Original Text:

Wisdom as a noun is a companion to those who will have her. The application of wisdom as a verb, however, is more than the ability to make a decision. The ability to make decisions is inherent in everyone. Many reasoning processes, however, are forward and while the results of application may appear advantageous, favor is a distinguishable flavor (unique characteristic) of a believer.

Commentary:

In this statement, the author discusses the difference between wisdom as a noun and wisdom as a verb. Wisdom as a noun is something that can be possessed or obtained, while the application of wisdom as a verb involves more than just making decisions. The author notes that the ability to make decisions is inherent in everyone, but it is the forward-thinking reasoning processes that lead to a distinguishable flavor of favor in believers. This means that wisdom is not just about making the right decision in the moment, but also about considering the long-term impact of one's actions and decisions.

Reflective Question:

How can we cultivate the ability to apply wisdom in our decision-making process, taking into account the long-term impact of our actions and decisions?

Original Text:

Wisdom, then, precedes the appropriate extrinsic or intrinsic application of knowledge (clean hands) to a situation, to manifest one's motive (pure heart). For the believer, Wisdom's presence is a constant companion to those becoming more self-aware of God's delight and Wisdom's rejoicing; her pleasure being with the decisions or actions of the sons of men.

Commentary:

In this statement, the author emphasizes the importance of wisdom in guiding and directing one's actions toward a pure and noble purpose. The application of knowledge with clean hands and a pure heart, which are the qualities of righteousness and genuine intentions, is crucial for manifesting one's motives in a positive manner. The author also notes that for believers, wisdom is a constant companion, and its presence brings delight to God and rejoicing to wisdom itself. The application of wisdom in decision-making and actions is a pleasing experience for both the individual and God.

Reflective Question:

How can we cultivate a deeper understanding of wisdom as a constant companion in our lives, and how can we apply it to our decisions and actions to bring delight to God and wisdom's rejoicing?

Original Text:

As she was from the beginning, so Wisdom is with the believer before an application; her presence glorifies God and assures favor of the Lord for those who listen to her, watch for her, lean on her, and apply her guidance.

Commentary:

This statement emphasizes the idea that Wisdom is always present with the believer, even before it is applied to a specific situation. The author notes that Wisdom's presence is a constant companion to those who actively seek it and apply its guidance. This companionship not only brings glory to God but also assures the favor of the Lord for those who follow Wisdom's direction. The use of the verbs "listen," "watch," "lean," and "apply" suggests that gaining wisdom requires active participation and engagement, rather than passive acceptance.

Reflective Question:

How can we actively seek and apply Wisdom's guidance in our daily lives, and how can this bring us closer to God and assure His favor?

Conclusion: Favor of the Lord

This chapter has highlighted the importance of wisdom in obtaining God's favor. The author emphasizes that wisdom is not something that can be obtained superficially but rather requires an inward journey of self-reflection and introspection. The chapter has also discussed the difference between having wisdom as a noun and applying it as a verb, emphasizing the importance of wisdom in decision-making for believers. Furthermore, the chapter has emphasized that wisdom is a constant companion for believers, leading them towards actions that please God and obtain His favor.

In summary, this chapter has reminded us that to obtain favor with God, we must have wisdom. It is not just about making the right decision in the moment, but also considering the long-term impact of our actions and decisions. Wisdom requires personal investment in studying, observing, noticing, or experiencing something necessary or relevant to the individual. By doing so, we can develop a deeper understanding and application of wisdom for the good of ourselves and others.

Chapter 12

Love Thy Neighbor as Thy Self and Bear No False Witness

Zechariah 8:17; Matthew 12:37; Psalm 4:5

From the collective synthesis of the above scriptures, one learns the value of a neighbor. If one is to honor God, one must love neighbor and abhor speaking wrong statements; for that which is spoken both helps and hurts our ability to trust in God and to do what is right.

The Bible is replete with scriptures that direct in how to live honorably. By living honorably, God receives glory, and He increases our worth toward humanity.

However, if we perceive evil in our hearts against our neighbor, there is the harboring of malice. Malice is the desire to cause harm to another or others, or to see somebody in pain. Malice estoppels prayers and praises because the righteous nature of prayers and praises is inconsistent with thoughts to hurt or harm another. Prayers and praises are before God. His receipt of prayers and praises justify; his rejection condemns. This is not the case where license toward righteousness prevails for sake of correction. Thus, one need not endure wrong actions of neighbors but must intervene for the good of all.

When and where there is need to arrest a neighborly situation, the action must be in the open and without malice intent. Such intervention is a sacrifice of righteousness in that risking friendship gives way to the greater good or the action will arrest a situation before it gels worst. Righteous intervention does what is right to correct a situation and after intervening, one's trust in God is the confidence of gaining rather than losing a neighbor.

It is, therefore, clear that expressions before God and toward neighbor(s) are interrelated and by words, one is justified or condemned.

Introduction: Love Thy Neighbor as Thy Self and Bear No False Witness

The commandment to love thy neighbor as thyself and bear no false witness is a central theme in many religious traditions, including Judaism and Christianity. The scriptures provide clear guidance on how to live an honorable life, which includes loving our neighbors and speaking truthfully. However, if we harbor malice towards our neighbors, it can hinder our ability to trust in God and live righteously. This chapter will explore the importance of loving our neighbors, speaking truthfully, and intervening for the greater good when necessary. We will also examine the relationship between our expressions before God and towards our neighbors, and how they are interrelated. Ultimately, by living honorably and loving our neighbors, we bring glory to God and increase our worth towards humanity.

Zechariah 8:17:

And let none of you imagine evil in your hearts against his neighbor; and love no false oath: for all these are things that I hate, saith the Lord.

Matthew 12:37:

For by thy words thou shalt be justified, and by thy words thou shalt be condemned.

Psalm 4:5:

Offer the sacrifices of righteousness, and put your trust in the Lord.

Original Text:

From the collective synthesis of the above scriptures, one learns the value of a neighbor. If one is to honor God, one must love neighbor and abhor speaking wrong statements; for that which is spoken both helps and hurts our ability to trust in God and to do what is right.

Commentary:

This statement highlights the value of a neighbor in honoring God. The collective synthesis of the above scriptures suggests that loving one's neighbor is an essential aspect of following God's commandments. This underscores the importance of treating others with respect and kindness, even when they are different from us.

The statement also emphasizes the power of words in helping or hurting our ability to trust in God and do what is right. Words have the ability to uplift and inspire, but they can also tear down and destroy. This is why it is important to be mindful of what we say and how we say it, as our words have the power to shape our relationships with others and our relationship with God.

In order to honor God, it is important to cultivate a spirit of love towards others and to strive to speak truthfully and kindly. By doing so, we can create an atmosphere of trust and mutual respect that enables us to live in harmony with our neighbors and with God.

Reflective Question:

How do you show love to your neighbors in your daily life? In what ways can you be more mindful of the words you speak and the impact they have on others and your relationship with God?

Original Text:
The Bible is replete with scriptures that direct in how to live honorably. By living honorably, God receives glory, and He increases our worth toward humanity.

Commentary:
This statement highlights the importance of living honorably according to the teachings of the Bible. The Bible contains numerous scriptures that provide guidance on how to live a life that is pleasing to God and beneficial to humanity. By following these teachings, we can live in a way that honors God and benefits others. This can lead to a sense of purpose and fulfillment in life, as well as a positive impact on those around us.

Living honorably also brings glory to God. By living according to His teachings, we demonstrate our love and reverence for Him. This can inspire others to seek a relationship with God and lead to an increased understanding of His love and grace. It also allows us to be a positive influence on those around us, as we model the values and behaviors that are pleasing to God.

Additionally, living honorably can increase our worth toward humanity. When we live in a way that benefits others, we become a valuable asset to our communities and society as a whole. This can lead to greater respect, trust, and admiration from others, as well as opportunities to make a positive impact in the world.

Reflective Question:
What specific teachings or principles from the Bible do you strive to follow in your daily life? How have these teachings impacted your relationships with others and your overall sense of purpose and fulfillment?

Original Text:

However, if we perceive evil in our hearts against our neighbor, there is the harboring of malice. Malice is the desire to cause harm to another or others, or to see somebody in pain. Malice estoppels prayers and praises because the righteous nature of prayers and praises is inconsistent with thoughts to hurt or harm another. Prayers and praises are before God. His receipt of prayers and praises justify; his rejection condemns. This is not the case where license toward righteousness prevails for sake of correction. Thus, one need not endure wrong actions of neighbors but must intervene for the good of all.

Commentary:

The statement highlights the negative impact of harboring malice towards our neighbors. Malice is the desire to cause harm or see someone in pain, and when we hold onto these negative feelings, it can prevent us from praying and praising God in a righteous manner. Our prayers and praises should be consistent with our desire for good and should not be tainted by malicious thoughts.

The statement also suggests that God receives our prayers and praises and either justifies or condemns them. This implies that the way we think and act towards others has a direct impact on our relationship with God. If we are harboring malice towards others, it will affect the quality of our prayers and praises and may prevent them from being heard or received by God.

However, the statement also acknowledges that there may be times when we need to intervene in the actions of our neighbors for the good of all. This suggests that we have a responsibility to help others when we can, even if it means correcting their behavior. It is important to approach these situations with a spirit of righteousness and a desire for the good of all involved.

Reflective Question:
Have you ever experienced the negative impact of harboring malice towards someone? How has this affected your relationship with God? How can you approach situations of correcting the behavior of others with a spirit of righteousness and a desire for the good of all involved?

Original Text:
When and where there is need to arrest a neighborly situation, the action must be in the open and without malice intent. Such intervention is a sacrifice of righteousness in that risking friendship gives way to the greater good or the action will arrest a situation before it gels worst. Righteous intervention does what is right to correct a situation and after intervening, one's trust in God is the confidence of gaining rather than losing a neighbor.

Commentary:
This statement emphasizes the importance of righteous intervention in neighborly situations that may require correction. It suggests that such actions should be taken openly, without any malice intent, and with a focus on the greater good rather than personal gain or preservation of friendship. The willingness to risk a friendship in order to correct a situation demonstrates a sacrifice of righteousness, which is an act of putting what is right above personal interests.

This sacrificial action of intervening in a neighborly situation may be necessary to prevent the situation from getting worse. It also demonstrates trust in God and confidence in gaining, rather than losing, a neighbor. This confidence is rooted in the belief that God rewards righteous actions and that ultimately, doing what is right will lead to positive outcomes.

This statement highlights the importance of balancing the desire for neighborly relationships with the need for righteous intervention. It suggests that in some cases, it may be necessary to risk a friendship in order to do what is right and ensure the greater good for all involved.

Reflective Question:

Have you ever had to intervene in a neighborly situation for the greater good? How did you approach the situation, and what motivated you to take action? How did the outcome affect your relationship with your neighbor, and did you feel confident in your decision to intervene?

Original Text:

It is, therefore, clear that expressions before God and toward neighbor(s) are interrelated and by words, one is justified or condemned.

Commentary:

This statement highlights the importance of our words and how they relate to our relationship with God and our neighbors. As human beings, we have the ability to speak words and express ourselves, but with that ability comes great responsibility. Our words have the power to build up or tear down, to heal or harm, to encourage or discourage.

In the context of our relationship with God, our words are a reflection of our heart and our faith. In the book of Matthew, Jesus said, "Out of the abundance of the heart the mouth speaks" (Matthew 12:34). This means that what we say is a reflection of what is in our hearts. If our hearts are filled with love, grace, and kindness, our words will reflect that. If our hearts are filled with anger, bitterness, and hatred, our words will reflect that as well.

Our words also have a significant impact on our relationship with our neighbors. Proverbs 18:21 says, "Death and life are in the power of the tongue, and those who love it will eat its fruit." This means that our words have the power to bring life and blessings or death and curses to our relationships with others. When we speak words of kindness, encouragement, and respect, we build up our neighbors and strengthen our relationships. When we speak words of anger, criticism, and disrespect, we tear down our neighbors and damage our relationships.

Ultimately, our words have eternal consequences. In the book of Matthew, Jesus said, "But I say to you that for every idle word man may speak, they will give account of it in the day of judgment. For by your words, you will be justified, and by your words, you will be condemned" (Matthew 12:36-37). This means that our words have the power to either justify or condemn us before God.

Reflective Question:

What steps can you take to ensure that your words reflect love, kindness, and respect for both God and your neighbors? How can you be intentional about using your words to build up and strengthen your relationships with others?

Conclusion: Love Thy Neighbor as Thy Self and Bear No False Witness

The conclusion of this chapter emphasizes the importance of loving our neighbors, speaking truthfully, intervening for the greater good, and the power of our words. The collective synthesis of the scriptures highlights the significance of treating others with respect and kindness, as well as being mindful of the impact our words have on others and our relationship with God. This requires a willingness to sacrifice personal interests for the greater good and to approach situations with a spirit of righteousness. Our words are not only a reflection of our heart and faith but also have the power to either build up or tear down our relationships with others and our relationship with God. Ultimately, living an honorable life that includes loving our neighbors and speaking truthfully brings glory to God and increases our worth towards humanity.

Chapter 13

Tears: A Reminder of What Will Come

Revelation 21:4

There will be no need for tears when the former things pass away.

Several years ago, God revealed that tears are a manifestation of His presence with me. According to this verse, there will be no need for a manifestation in that we will be with Him.

It is also noteworthy of the incidences that curse tears: death, sorrow, crying, and pain; however, there is no mention of tears of joy. Perhaps "tears of joy" is a misnomer or an anomaly known beyond the catalyst from which tears flow.

For example, generally, when a person is very excited, he/she will clap, jump, run, or even dance, and the latter without music. So it is that tears can be summoned during joyful times and tears, primarily, express loss, regret, wailing, or hurt.

Death, sorrow, crying, and pain have not an audience before God. Man knew these things on the introduction of sin upon humankind. Why then do many hold on to the things of this time, place, and space when death, sorrow, crying and pain create barriers to the original creation?

The promise is clear that He shall wipe away all tears, and all means all.

Introduction: Tears: A Reminder of What Will Come

The concept of tears is one that is often associated with sorrow and pain. However, as this chapter explores, tears can also be a manifestation of God's presence with us. Drawing inspiration from Revelation 21:4, the author notes that there will be no need for tears when the former things pass away, and we are reunited with God. The chapter delves into the various incidences that curse tears, including death, sorrow, crying, and pain, and asks why many still hold onto these things when they create barriers to the original creation. The promise of the verse is clear: God shall wipe away all tears, offering comfort and hope to those who suffer. Ultimately, this chapter invites readers to consider the role of tears in their lives, and to find comfort in the promise of God's presence and restoration.

Revelation 21:4:

"And God shall wipe away all tears from their eyes; and there shall be no more death, neither sorrow, nor crying, neither shall there be any more pain: for the former things are passed away."

Original Text:

There will be no need for tears when the former things pass away.

Commentary:

This statement from Revelation 21:4 speaks to the promise of a future without tears. It suggests that the current state of tears is linked to the former things, which will pass away. This implies that tears are a temporary condition and that there is a hope for a future where they will no longer be necessary. This promise is a source of comfort and hope for believers who may be experiencing pain, grief, or loss that leads to tears.

Reflective Question:

What are some ways we can hold onto hope for a future without tears, even in the midst of pain and suffering?

Original Text:

Several years ago, God revealed that tears are a manifestation of His presence with me. According to this verse, there will be no need for a manifestation in that we will be with Him.

Commentary:

This statement shares a personal experience of the author in which they discovered that tears can be a manifestation of God's presence. However, the author notes that according to Revelation 21:4, there will be no need for such a manifestation in the new heaven and earth, as we will be with Him directly. This statement reminds us that while tears may be a reminder of God's presence in our lives, they are not the ultimate expression of our connection with Him. The promise of being in His presence fully and directly is a powerful and comforting one.

Reflective Question:

How can we cultivate a deeper awareness of God's presence in our lives beyond the experience of tears, and what does it mean to be with Him directly in the new heaven and earth?

Original Text:

It is also noteworthy of the incidences that curse tears: death, sorrow, crying, and pain; however, there is no mention of tears of joy. Perhaps "tears of joy" is a misnomer or an anomaly known beyond the catalyst from which tears flow.

Commentary:

This statement draws attention to the nature of tears and how they are often associated with negative emotions and experiences such as death, sorrow, crying, and pain. However, there is no mention of tears of joy, which suggests that tears are not always a sign of sadness or distress. The author suggests that "tears of joy" may be a misnomer or an anomaly that goes beyond the reason for which tears flow. This raises interesting questions about the emotional and physical response of tears, and whether they are purely a result of negative experiences or if they can also be a response to positive ones.

Reflective Question:

Have you ever experienced tears of joy? What do you think is the significance of such a response and how does it relate to the experience itself?

Original Text:

For example, generally, when a person is very excited, he/she will clap, jump, run, or even dance, and the latter without music. So it is that tears can be summoned during joyful times and tears, primarily, express loss, regret, wailing, or hurt.

Commentary:

This statement presents a contrast between tears of joy and tears of sadness, highlighting the fact that tears are often associated with negative emotions. The author suggests that tears of joy may be an anomaly, as they are not mentioned in the Bible alongside other instances that cause tears, such as death, sorrow, crying, and pain. However, the author notes that tears can also be summoned during joyful times, much like how a person may clap, jump, or dance in excitement. While tears are often associated with expressions of loss, regret, wailing, or hurt, they can also be a natural response to overwhelming emotions, whether positive or negative.

Reflective Question:

Have you ever experienced tears of joy or found yourself crying during a moment of great happiness or excitement? How did that experience differ from tears shed during a moment of sadness or grief?

Original Text:

Death, sorrow, crying, and pain have not an audience before God. Man knew these things on the introduction of sin upon humankind. Why then do many hold to the things of this time, place, and space when death, sorrow, crying and pain create barriers to the original creation?

Commentary:

The author of this statement highlights the paradox of human attachment to things that are inherently flawed and lead to pain and suffering. Death, sorrow, crying, and pain are a result of sin entering the world, and they were not present in the original creation. However, despite this knowledge, many people continue to hold onto these things and create barriers to the original state of creation, which was perfect and without these negative elements. The author suggests that this attachment may be due to a lack of understanding of the true nature of the original creation and the promise of a future free from death, sorrow, crying, and pain.

Reflective Question:
How can we overcome our attachment to things that lead to death, sorrow, crying, and pain and embrace the promise of a future free from these negative elements?

Original Text:
The promise is clear that He shall wipe away all tears, and all means all.

Commentary:
This statement refers to the promise in Revelation 21:4 that God will wipe away every tear from our eyes and there will be no more death, mourning, crying, or pain. The promise of the elimination of these negative emotions and experiences is a powerful reminder of the hope and comfort that is available to believers in God. The phrase "all means all" emphasizes that there will be no exceptions to this promise and that it applies to every individual who chooses to follow God.

Reflective Question:
How does the promise of God wiping away all tears bring comfort and hope in times of sorrow and pain? How can we hold onto this promise and trust in God's faithfulness in the midst of difficult circumstances?

Conclusion: Tears: A Reminder of What Will Come

The concept of tears is a complex one, as explored in this chapter. While tears are often associated with negative emotions such as death, sorrow, crying, and pain, they can also be a manifestation of God's presence or a response to overwhelming joy or emotion. This paradox raises questions about the nature of tears and their significance in our lives. However, the promise of Revelation 21:4 is clear: there will be no more tears, death, sorrow, crying, or pain in the new heaven and earth. This promise offers hope and comfort to believers who may be experiencing difficult circumstances. As we reflect on the role of tears in our lives, may we hold onto the promise of God's faithfulness and the restoration of all things in the future.

Chapter 14

Prayer: A Conversation Without Covetousness

Hebrews 13:5

The Book of Hebrews is an excellent listing of behavioral tips essential to things being well with one's soul. A closer examination, however, reveals tremendous truths; one in particular is the above verse herein paraphrased:

Let your prayers be without yearning and be content with what you have: for as I have said, I will never depart from you, nor will I abandon you in prayer.

This verse illustrates the intra-relations of idle speech and prayer in the realm of covetous conversation; a speaking filled with desire for someone else's possessions or the wanting strongly of things not possessed, in spite of what is possessed. God hears both idle speech and prayer; covetous conversation suggesting a lack of appreciation for the tremendous value God bestows in the provisions of individual and customized blessings. Instead, in creeps an ungodly personality of ignorance and negligible thoughts about the things of Jehovah-Jirah; these thoughts, are expressed as a strong desire tinged with sadness (yearnings) that take center stage rather than supplications (humble requests to one having the power to grant requests) and invariably become an offense to blessings.

As it is with appreciation and use of spiritual gifts, the capacity can be diversified and its' application exponential, so it is with the appreciation of blessings. However, a spiritual gift left without appreciation and application is a gift lost to one and bestowed upon another. Thus, an offense to blessings minimizes the mindset and distorts realities such that deterioration manifests and value in the blessing is lost to neglect.

Allah is aware of what we need, both individually and collectively. It seems when we have thoughts otherwise about his omniscience, omnipresence, and omnipotence, the focus of conversation ought not be Idle speech, but prayer for the restoration of good and pleasing thoughts. For it is "with God" that the desires of our heart are known, and He alone can bestow that which is asked; the believers' portion being in alignment with His will and to His glory.

It is, therefore, one's level of contentment with such things as "ye have" that is the litmus test to one's alignment with Allah. Where there is a perpendicular alignment of hope engaged along a horizontal plane of desire, the interlacing bears witness to His promise to never leave us nor forsake our prayer.

Plainly stated and in line with His being with us "all the way", the promise is He will never leave us alone, nor forsake to hear our prayers.

Introduction: Prayer: A Conversation without Covetousness

The Book of Hebrews provides behavioral tips for a healthy soul, including the importance of praying without covetousness, as noted in Hebrews 13:5. This chapter explores the relationship between idle speech, prayer, and covetousness and the significance of humbly requesting blessings instead of yearning for them. It emphasizes the importance of contentment and alignment with Allah, reminding readers that their level of contentment is a litmus test of their alignment with God. Prayer is an opportunity to align desires with God's will and glory, free from covetousness, and to witness God's promise to never leave or forsake them.

Hebrews 13:5:

"Let your conversation be without covetousness; and be content with such things as ye have: for he hath said, I will never leave thee, nor forsake thee."

Original Text:

The Book of Hebrews is an excellent listing of behavioral tips essential to things being well with one's soul. A closer examination, however, reveals tremendous truths, one, in particular, is the above verse herein paraphrased:

Let your prayers be without yearning and be content with what you have: for as I have said, I will never depart from you, nor will I abandon you in prayer.

This verse illustrates the intra-relations of idle speech and prayer in the realm of covetous conversation; a speaking filled with desire for someone else's possessions or the wanting strongly of things not possessed, in spite of what is possessed. God hears both idle speech and prayer; covetous conversation suggesting a lack of appreciation for the tremendous value God bestows in the provisions of individual and customized blessings. Instead, in creeps an ungodly personality of ignorance and negligible thoughts about the things of Jehovah-Jirah; these thoughts, are expressed as a strong desire tinged with sadness (yearnings) that take center stage rather than supplications (humble requests to one having the power to grant requests) and invariably become on offense to blessings.

Commentary:

The above statement highlights the importance of prayer without yearning and being content with what one has, as illustrated in Hebrews 13:5. It emphasizes the relationship between idle speech, covetous conversation, and prayer, noting that covetous conversation can suggest a lack of appreciation for God's provisions and blessings. The author points out that God hears both idle speech and prayer, and covetous conversation can take center stage in the form of a strong desire tinged with sadness, which becomes an offense to blessings.

The author's emphasis on the intra-relations between idle speech and prayer is significant in that it suggests that our words matter in the spiritual realm. Idle speech, which can include covetous conversation, also suggests a lack of appreciation for what God has provided and can hinder one's prayer life. In contrast, prayer that is humble, without yearning, and content with what one has, can align one's desires with God's will and lead to blessings.

The author's statement also highlights the importance of recognizing and appreciating individual and customized blessings. It is easy to focus on what one does not have or yearn for things that others possess, but this mindset can lead to a lack of gratitude and contentment. By being content with what one has and recognizing the value of individual blessings, one can better appreciate and utilize what God has provided.

Reflective Question:

How can one cultivate a mindset of gratitude and contentment in prayer and daily life in a culture that often values material possessions and societal status; such a reality makes it challenging to avoid covetous conversation and focus on individual blessings?

Original Text:

As it is with appreciation and use of spiritual gifts, the capacity diversified and application exponential, so it is with the appreciation of blessings. However, a spiritual gift left without appreciation and application is a gift lost to one and bestowed upon another. Thus, an offense to blessings minimizes the mindset and distorts realities such that deterioration manifests and value in the blessing is lost to neglect.

Commentary:

This statement draws a parallel between the appreciation and use of spiritual gifts and the appreciation of blessings. The author suggests that, like spiritual gifts, blessings have the capacity to diversify and exponentially increase in their application. However, when a blessing is left unappreciated and unused, it is lost to the individual and may be bestowed upon another who is more appreciative. The author notes that neglecting blessings can lead to a distorted reality, where the value of the blessing is lost and deterioration manifests. This statement emphasizes the importance of recognizing and appreciating the blessings in our lives, as neglecting them can lead to a loss of their value and potential.

Reflective Question:

What are some ways we can cultivate an attitude of appreciation for the blessings in our lives and avoid neglecting them? How can we ensure that we are using our blessings in ways that align with God's will and bring glory to Him?

Original Text:

Allah is aware of what we need, both individually and collectively. It seems when we have thoughts otherwise about his omniscience, omnipresence, and omnipotence, the focus of conversation ought to not be Idle speech but prayer for the restoration of good and pleasing thoughts. For it is In God that the desires of our heart are known, and He alone can bestow that which is asked; the believers' portion being in alignment with His will and to His glory.

Commentary:

This statement emphasizes the importance of prayer and aligning our desires with God's will. The author notes that Allah is aware of our individual and collective needs and that we should have faith in His omniscience, omnipresence, and omnipotence. When we have thoughts that suggest otherwise, the author encourages us to turn to prayer instead of idle speech. Through prayer, we can restore good and pleasing thoughts and align our desires with God's will.

The author also highlights the importance of asking for what we need and relying on God's ability to provide for us. The believers' portion is in alignment with God's will and to His glory, which suggests that when we align our desires with God's will, we are more likely to receive what we need and glorify God in the process.

Reflective Question:

How can we cultivate a deeper trust in God's omniscience, omnipresence, and omnipotence, and how can we ensure that our desires are aligned with His will in our prayers?

Original Text:

It is, therefore, one's level of contentment with such things as ye have that is the litmus test to one's alignment with Allah. Where there is a perpendicular alignment of hope engaged along a horizontal plane of desire, the interlacing bears witness to His promise to never leave us nor forsake our prayer.

Commentary:

In this statement, the author emphasizes the importance of contentment as a litmus test of one's alignment with Allah. The focus is not on the quantity of blessings, but rather on the level of contentment with what one has been given. When individuals are content with what they have, they align them-selves with Allah's will and plan for their lives. This alignment creates a "perpendicular alignment of hope" and a "horizontal plane of desire," where individuals' hopes are in line with their desires. This alignment results in a powerful interlacing that bears witness to Allah's promise to never leave nor forsake them in prayer.

This statement highlights the importance of trust and faith in Allah's plan for our lives. When we are content with what we have and align our hopes and desires with His will, we open ourselves up to receiving His blessings and experiencing His presence in our lives. The challenge, however, is to maintain this contentment in the face of difficulties and challenges that may arise. It requires a deep trust in Allah's wisdom and goodness, and a willingness to surrender our own desires to His plan.

Reflective Question:

How can we cultivate contentment in our lives and align our hopes and desires with Allah's will, even in the face of difficulties and challenges? How can we maintain this alignment and trust in His plan for our lives?

Original Text:

Plainly stated and in line with His being with us "all the way", the promise is He will never leave us alone, nor forsake to hear our prayers.

Commentary:

This statement reiterates the promise of God's constant presence and faithfulness to those who pray and seek Him. It emphasizes the idea that no matter what the circumstances may be, God will always be there for His believers, listening to their prayers and providing comfort and guidance. The statement is also a reminder that prayer is a powerful tool for communicating with God and strengthening the relationship between believers and their Creator.

Reflective Question:

How does the promise of God's constant presence and faithfulness impact your personal prayer life? How can you deepen your trust in God's faithfulness and seek to align your prayers with His will?

Conclusion: Prayer: A Conversation Without Covetousness

The importance of prayer without covetousness is highlighted in the Book of Hebrews. This chapter explored the relationship between idle speech, prayer, and covetousness, emphasizing the significance of humbly requesting blessings instead of yearning for them. The author stressed the importance of contentment and alignment with Allah, reminding readers that their level of contentment is a litmus test of their alignment with God. Prayer is an opportunity to align desires with God's will and glory, free from covetousness, and to witness God's promise to never leave or forsake believers.

The chapter also emphasized the importance of recognizing and appreciating individual and customized blessings. Neglecting blessings can lead to a distorted reality, where the value of the blessing is lost, and deterioration manifests. The author drew a parallel between the appreciation and use of spiritual gifts and the appreciation of blessings. Like spiritual gifts, blessings have the capacity to diversify and exponentially increase in their application. However, when a blessing is left unappreciated and unused, it is lost to the individual and may be bestowed upon another who is more appreciative.

The statement further highlighted the importance of prayer and aligning our desires with God's will. Allah is aware of our individual and collective needs, and we should have faith in His omniscience, omnipresence, and omnipotence. Through prayer, we can restore good and pleasing thoughts and align our desires with God's will. The focus is not on the quantity of blessings, but rather on the level of contentment with what one has been given. When individuals are content with what they have, they align themselves with Allah's will and plan for their lives.

In conclusion, prayer without covetousness is an essential aspect of a healthy soul. It is an opportunity to align desires with God's will and glory, free from covetousness, and to witness God's promise to never leave or forsake believers. The key is to cultivate contentment and align our hopes and desires with Allah's will. Through deep trust in Allah's wisdom and goodness, we can surrender our own desires to His plan and experience His constant presence and faithfulness.

Chapter 15

From Everlasting to Everlasting: It is Profitable

Psalm 90:2 & 4

You are God and have always been God. You are the one who gives life to all things. As you desired, the mountains were born and the earth and worlds were brought forth. From eternity, time, and back to eternity you are God. You were, have and will always be God.

You are not restricted by time and you are not confined by the boundaries of human imaginings. Even time does not capture surprise for you and while it may seem to have a beginning and an end, your realm of existence is far greater and without boundaries. Your day is far greater than my day and your night greater than my night. As these pass from me, your eternity is endless and without human measure; in your sight do I crave to belong and your majesty will forever be in awe to my understanding.

To weary you with my plans is a telling weakness of my imagination. For the realm of God requires that I work and not weary with plans, hopes, and dreams. From everlasting to everlasting, you have designed, determined and destined that which is good and profitable to me.

Introduction: From Everlasting to Everlasting: It is Profitable

The Book of Psalms is a collection of poems and songs that express a wide range of emotions and experiences, from praise and thanksgiving to lament and despair. In Psalm 90, the author reflects on the eternal nature of God and the brevity of human life. The chapter begins with a declaration of God's everlasting existence and the author's acknowledgement of his power to give life to all things. The author marvels at the fact that God is not confined by time or human limitations and that His plans and purposes for humanity are good and profitable. This chapter reminds us of the importance of recognizing God's eternal nature and trusting in His plans for our lives, even when we do not fully understand them. It is a call to focus on the eternal, rather than the temporal, and to trust in the goodness and faithfulness of God.

Psalm 90:2 & 4 (KJV):

2 Before the mountains were brought forth, or ever thou hadst formed the earth and the world, even from everlasting to everlasting, thou art God.

4 For a thousand years in thy sight are but as yesterday when it is past, and as a watch in the night.

Original Text:

You are God and have always been God. You are the one who gives life to all things. As you desired, the mountains were born and the earth and worlds were brought forth. From eternity, time, and back to eternity you are God. You were, have and will always be God.

Commentary:

This statement expresses a deep sense of awe and reverence for God's eternal nature and power as the Creator of all things. The author acknowledges that God has always existed and will always exist, and that He is the one who gives life to all things. The author also highlights God's role in the creation of the mountains, the earth, and the worlds, emphasizing that God's desires and will are the driving force behind all of creation. By acknowledging God's eternal nature and creative power, the author is positioning God as the ultimate authority and source of life.

Reflective Question:

How does acknowledging God's eternal nature and creative power impact your personal faith and relationship with Him? In what ways does recognizing God as the ultimate authority and source of life shape your understanding of the world and your place in it?

Original Text:

You are not restricted by time and you are not confined by the boundaries of human imaginings. Even time does not capture surprise for you and while it may seem to have a beginning and an end, your realm of existence is far greater and without boundaries. Your day is far greater than my day and your night greater than my night. As these will pass for me, your eternity is endless and without human measure, in your sight do I crave to belong and your majesties will forever be in awe to my understanding.

Commentary:

This statement emphasizes the vastness and infinity of God's existence, beyond the limitations of human understanding. The author notes that God is not restricted by time or human boundaries and that even time does not surprise Him. The statement highlights the fact that while our days and nights are limited, God's eternity is endless and without measure. The author expresses a deep desire to belong to God's realm of existence and to be in awe of His majesty forever.

Reflective Question:

How can we cultivate a deeper appreciation for the vastness and infinity of God's existence, beyond the limitations of our human understanding? How can we come to a greater understanding of God's eternal nature and align our desires with His will?

Original Text:

To weary you with my plans is a telling weakness of my imagination. For the realm of God requires that I work and not weary with plans, hopes, and dreams. From «everlasting to everlasting", you have designed, determined and destined that which is good and profitable for me.

Commentary:

In this statement, the author acknowledges the limitations of human imagination and the vastness of God's realm of existence. The author recognizes that trying to burden God with plans and dreams is a weakness in one's own imagination, as God's plans for our lives are already determined and designed from everlasting to everlasting. The author emphasizes the importance of working in alignment with God's plans, rather than relying solely on our own plans, hopes, and dreams. Trusting in God's plan can lead to a sense of peace and contentment in life, knowing that He has designed what is good and profitable for us.

Reflective Question:

How do you balance your own plans, hopes, and dreams with the knowledge that God has already designed what is good and profitable for you? How can you learn to work in alignment with His plans for your life and trust in His timing, even when it may not align with your own desires?

Conclusion: From Everlasting to Everlasting: It is Profitable

Psalm 90 reminds us of the eternal nature of God and the brevity of human life. The author marvels at the fact that God is not confined by time or human limitations and that His plans and purposes for humanity are good and profitable. The chapter is a call to focus on the eternal, rather than the temporal, and to trust in the goodness and faithfulness of God. The three verses discussed in this chapter highlight God's eternal nature and creative power, as well as the importance of working in alignment with His plans for our lives. By acknowledging God's infinite nature and trusting in His plans, we can find peace and contentment in life, knowing that He has designed what is good and profitable for us.

As we reflect on Psalm 90, we are invited to consider the vastness and infinity of God's existence and the importance of aligning our plans with His. How can we deepen our understanding of God's eternal nature and trust in His plans for our lives? How can we learn to work in alignment with His will, even when it may not align with our own desires? These are questions that require deep reflection and a willingness to surrender our plans to God's infinite wisdom and guidance.

Chapter 16

A Confession of
Affections

Colossians 3:2

At any time, one can be consumed with the cares of this world. These cares, while important, ought not to be the essence of life. Where panic, depression, anxiety and other negative forms of living tend to dominate, then one's affections are on the things on earth rather than having affection on things above.

God is the maker and creator of all that is on the earth. He has a plan and knows the outcome of His plan. It is interesting that many forget that He started things and he will finish things. There is nothing that escapes God. When the cares of this earth tend to dominate, it is a good thing to consider that which has its being in nature.

Every day the birds of the air find nourishment. Every day a tree falls and while we may not hear the sound, God knows the tree has fallen. Every day the sun comes out and sets to bring the night. At no time must we stop to adjust the rhythm, the seasons or rewind time. Every day there is sufficient hydrogen, oxygen and other gases necessary to sustain the air we breathe. Everyday God takes us through the day; some experiencing the beginning of the dash of life, others ending the dash of life.

The reason man tends to get entangled with worry, frustration and anxiety is because he/she fails to consider God in all things. I am currently facing the end of my time at a place of employment where I thought I would retire. God told me years ago that retirement was not my concern. So, while I accepted the absence of retirement as a goal, there remained the need to be employed.

The good thing is I am not alone. Throughout the day, when anxiety creeps into mv space, the Spirit of the Lord intercedes and says, "You are not alone, I am here. Stay focused." Thus and sometimes fear tries to enter into the holy substance of my being. My faith alone speaks back quickly to the unknown and says, ". When God says not to worry, then I don't worry.

I have not always known how to do this but time has shown me that no matter what happens, the concerns of the day will pass. What I think about is losing everything. God speaks back and reminds me that everything I have, He provided; that nothing will be lost. In other words: all that He has provided, he will protect and I will keep. What calm assurance His voice and this thought brings to a soul under seize.

It is a good thing to know and have God as the center of one's being. As the center, then whatever comes, there will remain loyalty, allegiance and commitment to focus toward that which God has commanded: To love the Lord thy God with all thy heart, mind, and strength, and to love thy neighbor as thy self are more than words, but a call to faith and a commitment to God's sovereignty.

Affections are for God and mankind; however, things distract and misplace affections.

Introduction: A Confession of Affections

The world we live in can be filled with cares and concerns that often dominate our thoughts and affections, causing anxiety, worry, and even depression. In Colossians 3:2, the Apostle Paul reminds us to set our minds on things above, rather than on earthly things. This chapter is a confession of affections, acknowledging the importance of keeping God at the center of our being, and aligning our thoughts and actions with His will.

The author notes that God is the creator of all things and has a plan that He is working, and it is only when we lose sight of this that we tend to become consumed with worry and anxiety. The author also reflects on experiences of facing the end of a long career and the uncertainties that come with it. Yet, through it all, the author finds comfort in knowing that God is present and providing, and that nothing will be lost.

This chapter reminds us of the importance of aligning our affections with God and loving Him with all our heart, mind, and strength, as well as loving our neighbors as ourselves. By keeping God at the center of our being, we can find peace and contentment, even in the midst of life's uncertainties and challenges.

Colossians 3:2 (NIV):

Set your minds on things above, not on earthly things.

Original Text:

At any time, one can be consumed with the cares of this world. These cares, while important, ought not to be the essence of life. Where panic, depression, anxiety and other negative forms of living tend to dominate, then one's affections are on the things on earth rather than having affection on things above.

Commentary:

The author begins by acknowledging that it is easy for individuals to become consumed with the cares of this world, which can lead to negative forms of living such as panic, depression, and anxiety. The author emphasizes that while these cares may be important, they should not be the essence of life. By allowing these negative forms of living to dominate, our affections are misplaced and directed towards things on earth rather than having affection for things above.

The statement encourages us to refocus our affections on God and the eternal, rather than being consumed by the temporary concerns of this world. This shift in perspective can lead to a sense of peace and contentment, knowing that our lives are centered on what truly matters in the grand scheme of things.

Reflective Question:

How do you prioritize your affections between the cares of this world and things above? What steps can you take to refocus your affections towards God and the eternal, even in the midst of life's challenges and struggles?

Original Text:

God is the maker and creator of all that is on the earth. He has a plan and knows the outcome of His plan. It is interesting that many forget that He started things and he will finish things. There is nothing that escapes God. When the cares of this earth tend to dominate, it is a good thing to consider that which has its' being in nature.

Commentary:

This statement highlights the importance of remembering God's role as the Creator of all things and the fact that He has a plan for His creation. The author emphasizes that nothing escapes God's knowledge and when the cares of this earth tend to dominate our thoughts, it is beneficial to consider the natural world around us as a reminder of God's power and sovereignty. By reflecting on the intricate design and order of nature, we can gain a greater appreciation for God's handiwork and the fact that He is in control.

Reflective Question:

In what ways can you take time to intentionally observe and appreciate the natural world around you as a reminder of God's power and sovereignty? How can reflecting on God's role as the Creator of all things help to shift your perspective away from the cares of this world and towards a deeper appreciation for His plan for your life?

Original Text:

Every day the birds of the air find nourishment. Every day a tree falls and while we may not hear the sound, God knows the tree has fallen. Every day the sun comes out and sets to bring the night. At no time must we stop to adjust the rhythm, the seasons or rewind time. Every day there is sufficient hydrogen, oxygen and other gases necessary to stock the air we breathe. Every day God takes us through the day; some experiencing the beginning of the dash of life, others ending the dash of life.

Commentary:

This statement highlights the consistent and dependable nature of God's creation. The author notes the everyday oc-currences in nature, such as birds finding nourishment and the sun rising and setting, and how they continue to happen without human interference. The author also acknowledges the inevitability of life and death, with some experiencing the beginning of life while others reach the end of their time on earth. By pointing to the consistency of nature and the cycles of life, the author emphasizes the dependability of God and the importance of trusting in His plan.

Reflective Question:

How does reflecting on the consistency and dependability of God's creation help us to trust in His plan for our lives? In what ways can we find peace and comfort in the cycles of nature and the inevitability of life and death? How can we cul-tivate a deeper appreciation for the dependability of God and His creation in our daily lives?

Original Text:

The reason man tends to get entangled with worry, frustration and anxiety is because he/she fails to consider God in all things. At the time of this writing, I was facing the end of my time at a place of employment where I thought I would retire. God told me years ago that retirement was not my concern. So, while I can accept the absence of retirement as a goal, there remained the need to be employed.

Commentary:

This statement highlights the importance of considering God in all aspects of life, particularly in times of worry and anxiety. The author shares a personal experience of facing the end of their time at a place of employment where retirement would be inevitable. Despite feeling uncertain about the future, the author trusted in God's plan and guidance. The author acknowledges that worrying and becoming entangled in anxiety can occur when we fail to consider God in all things.

Reflective Question:

In what ways do you tend to get entangled in worry and anxiety in your own life? How can you work on considering God in all things and trusting in His plan and guidance, even in uncertain times?

Original Text:

The good thing is I am not alone. Throughout the day, when anxiety creeps into my space, the Spirit of the Lord intercedes and says, "You are not alone, I am here. Stay focused. Thus, and sometimes fear tries to enter into the holy substance of my being. My faith alone speaks back quickly to the unknown and says, God knows and He has provided. He is more than enough. He has made me and knows who I am and how much I need him to make this time bearable. He has said to me, not to worry. When God says not to worry, then I don't worry. I have not always known how to do this, but time has shown me that no matter what happens, the concerns of the day will pass. What I think about is losing everything. God speaks back and reminds me that everything I have, He provided; that nothing will be lost. All that He has provided, he will protect and I will keep. What calm assurance His voice and this thought brings to a soul under seize.

Commentary:

The author shares a personal testimony of how their faith in God provides comfort and peace in times of anxiety and uncertainty. Even in the face of losing a job and the unknown future, the author trusts that God has a plan and will provide for needs. The author relies on the voice of the Holy Spirit to remind us that we are not alone and that God is with us, providing the necessary strength to stay focused and not give in to fear. This testimony encourages readers to trust in God's provision and to rely on His voice for guidance and comfort.

Reflective Question:

How does the author's testimony of relying on God's voice for comfort and assurance in times of anxiety and uncertainty inspire you in your own faith journey? How can you cultivate a deeper trust in God's provision and guidance in your own life?

Original Text:

It is a good thing to know and have God as the center of one's being. As the center, then whatever comes, there will remain loyalty, allegiance and commitment to focus toward that which God has commanded: To love the Lord thy God with all thy heart, mind, and strength, and to love thy neighbor as thy self.

Commentary:

This statement emphasizes the importance of having God as the center of one's being. When God is at the center, our affections, desires, and actions are aligned with His will and purpose. The author highlights the commandment to love God with all our heart, mind, and strength and to love our neighbor as ourselves. This commandment is not only a call to action, but also a call to a particular way of being in the world. When God is at the center, we are called to a life of loyalty, allegiance, and commitment to these commandments.

Reflective Question:

How can we ensure that God is at the center of our being? In what ways can we cultivate a deeper sense of loyalty, allegiance, and commitment to God and His commandments in our daily lives? How does prioritizing our relationship with God impact our relationships with others and our sense of purpose and meaning in life?

Original Text:
Affections are for God and mankind; things distract and misplace affections.

Commentary:
This statement highlights the importance of directing one's affections towards God and humanity, rather than becoming distracted and placing affections on material possessions or worldly concerns. By recognizing that true fulfillment and purpose comes from a relationship with God and serving others, the author is encouraging readers to prioritize their values and maintain a sense of focus in their lives. By doing so, they will not only experience a greater sense of meaning and purpose, but also avoid the pitfalls of becoming consumed by worldly distractions.

Reflective Question:
In what ways have you experienced the misplacement of affections in your own life? How can you redirect your focus towards God and serving others, in order to experience a greater sense of fulfillment and purpose?

Conclusion: A Confession of Affections

This chapter is a reflection on the importance of keeping God at the center of our lives, particularly during times of uncertainty, worry, and anxiety. The author reminds us of God's sovereignty and power as the Creator of all things, and encourages us to trust in His plan and provision for our lives. By refocusing our affections towards God and serving others, we can find peace and contentment, even in the midst of life's challenges.

The author's personal testimony serves as an inspiration and encouragement to readers, reminding us that we are not alone and that God is always present, providing comfort and guidance. The importance of prioritizing our relationship with God and serving others is emphasized as a means of avoiding the pitfalls of becoming consumed by worldly distractions.

As we reflect on this chapter, let us consider the ways in which we can redirect our focus towards God and serving others, and how doing so can bring a greater sense of purpose and fulfillment to our lives. May we all strive to keep God at the center of our being, and remain loyal, committed, and focused on His will and purpose for our lives.

Chapter 17

Pour Out Your Heart

Psalm 62:8

To trust in God is to have true rest from what is of greatest concern to you in a day. God provides and expects us to inhabit his presence, one day at a time. It is while the day is here that we are encouraged to "pour out our heart before Him."

To pour out one's heart is to state (and restate if necessary) that which seeks to rob the beauty from the day and leave one in a state that was not planned or desired by God. Each day is a blessed day. A day to reflect, a day to repent, a day to review, a day to keep, a day to take notice of God all that he has set before us. The pouring out, then, is an expression of hurt, pain, discomfort; anything that seeks to rob the day of what God has purposed. He is a refuge for us.

The reason the psalmist included the last sentence is because he understood the need for a refuge when one is pouring out his/her heart before the Lord. At these times, the pouring is a plea and the plea is directed to the One who can effectively address the need to "pour out the heart."

It is of no benefit to bemoan oppression or an oppressive state but rather, to pour out the heart to Him who is a safe place and will annul the situation; the result of which builds trust in God. When done consistently to redeem the day, then one's trust will manifest "at all times."

Introduction: Pour Out Your Heart

In Psalm 62:8, the Psalmist reminds us of the importance of pouring out our hearts before God. To trust in God is to have true rest from what concerns us the most each day. God provides and expects us to dwell in His presence, one day at a time. The act of pouring out one's heart before God is an expression of hurt, pain, discomfort, or anything that seeks to rob the day of what God has purposed. Each day is a blessed day, a day to reflect, repent, review, and take notice of God and all that He has set before us. Pouring out our hearts is a plea directed to the One who can effectively address our needs, and it builds trust in Him as our refuge. When done consistently, this act of pouring out our hearts to redeem the day can manifest trust in God at all times. In this chapter, we will explore the significance of pouring out our hearts before God and how it can deepen our relationship with Him.

Psalm 62:8

"Trust in him at all times; ye people, pour out your heart before him: God is a refuge for us. Selah."

Original Text:

To trust in God is to have true rest from what is of greatest concern to you in a day. God provides and expects us to inhabit his presence, one day at a time. It is while the day is here that we are encouraged to "pour out our heart before Him."

Commentary:

The statement highlights the importance of trust in God and finding true rest from the worries and concerns of daily life. Trusting in God means acknowledging that He is in control and that we can rely on Him to provide for our needs. The author emphasizes that God expects us to seek His presence and guidance each day, rather than trying to manage on our own. The act of pouring out our hearts before God is a powerful tool for finding peace and solace, as it allows us to express our concerns and fears to Him in a raw and honest way. This act of vulnerability fosters intimacy with God and deepens our trust in Him.

Reflective Question:

What are some of the greatest concerns you face on a daily basis? How can you cultivate a deeper sense of trust in God and rely on Him to provide for your needs? How can the act of pouring out your heart before God help you find true rest and peace in the midst of life's challenges and uncertainties?

Original Text:

To pour out one's heart is to state (and restate if necessary) that which seeks to rob the beauty from the day and leave one in a state that was not planned or desired by God. Each day is a blessed day. A day to reflect, a day to repent, a day to review, a day to keep, a day to take notice of God and all that he has set before us. The pouring out, then, is an expression of hurt, pain, discomfort; anything that seeks to rob the day of what God has purposed. He is a refuge for us.

Commentary:

This passage highlights the importance of pouring out our hearts before God. When we express our deepest feelings to Him, we acknowledge that God is our refuge and that He is in control of our lives. By doing so, we release our anxieties and fears to Him, and we allow Him to restore the beauty of our day. In pouring out our hearts, we recognize that each day is a gift from God and that we should take notice of everything He has set before us.

Reflective Question:

How often do you take the time to pour out your heart before God? Do you see each day as a blessing and an opportunity to reflect, repent, and review your life in light of God's purposes for you?

Original Text:

The reason the psalmist included the last sentence is because he understood the need for a refuge when one is pouring out his/ her heart before the Lord. At these times, the pouring is a plea and the plea is directed to the One who can effectively address the need to "pour out the heart."

Commentary:

The psalmist's inclusion of the last sentence in Psalm 62:8 highlights the importance of seeking refuge in God when we pour out our hearts before Him. Pouring out our hearts can be a vulnerable and emotional experience, and it is comforting to know that we have a safe place to turn to in God. The psalmist recognizes that God is the only one who can effectively address the needs we express when we pour out our hearts before Him.

This verse reminds us that we don't have to carry our burdens alone. We can take comfort in knowing that we can turn to God for refuge, comfort, and help. This should encourage us to pour out our hearts before God with sincerity, honesty, and faith, trusting that He will hear our prayers and provide for our needs.

Reflective Question:

How can you seek refuge in God when you are pouring out your heart to Him? What are some ways you can trust in God's goodness and provision, even in the midst of difficult circumstances?

Original Text:

It is of no benefit to bemoan oppression or an oppressive state but rather, to pour out the heart to Him who is a safe place and will annul the situation, and build trust. When done consistently to redeem the day, then one's trust will manifest "at all times."

Commentary:

This statement reminds us of the futility of complaining about difficult situations without taking action or seeking help from God. Instead, it encourages us to trust in God's ability to help us through our struggles and to pour out our hearts to Him in prayer. Pouring out our hearts to God helps us to acknowledge our struggles and trust in His power to help us overcome them. It builds our faith and helps us to develop a deeper relationship with God.

Reflective Question:

Do you find yourself complaining about your problems or pouring out your heart to God in prayer? What steps can you take to develop a deeper trust in God's ability to help you through your struggles?

Conclusion: Pour Out Your Heart

In Psalm 62:8, we are reminded to pour out our hearts before God and trust in Him at all times. Pouring out our hearts is an act of vulnerability and honesty that allows us to acknowledge our struggles and find solace in God as our refuge. Through this act, we can deepen our relationship with God and cultivate a deeper sense of trust in His ability to provide for our needs. It is essential to recognize that each day is a blessing and an opportunity to reflect, repent, review, and take notice of all that God has set before us. Pouring out our hearts consistently to redeem the day can manifest trust in God at all times. Let us make it a habit to pour out our hearts to God and trust in His goodness and provision in all circumstances.

Chapter 18

Know Thyself

Philippians 2:3

What a terrible thing it is when one is compelled toward rivalry or excessive boasting with individuals in the faith, to gain attention. Such behavior is without the expectation of a believer.

Self-examination begets honesty and honesty with one's own self builds self- confidence. This is a mystery. It is only when one can look from within and "know thy self", that one gains confidence. Where there is an absence of self-confidence there will be selfishness, and where there is selfishness, there also is self-centeredness. To this is added that a self-centered person reflects self-talk at its' worst extreme. This kind of self-talk negates the opportunity to share with others. When we share with one another, therein will be demonstrated self-centeredness and the esteeming of others better than ourselves.

It is not what we say to ourselves, but what others say about us that is the true measure of the inward self, presented outwardly. This outward presentation, where there is lowliness of mind or respectfulness toward others (love thy neighbor as thy self), that allows one to reconcile his or her own former state with one's present state, and promote the better good in those that are in the faith.

Introduction: Know Thy Self

In Philippians 2:3, we are reminded of the dangers of excessive boasting and rivalry within the faith. Such behavior is not expected of believers and can lead to selfishness and self-centeredness. It is only through self-examination and honesty with one's self that true self-confidence can be built. When we esteem others better than ourselves and share with one another, we demonstrate respectfulness and promote the better good in the faith. In this chapter, we will explore the importance of knowing oneself, and how it can lead to humility, respectfulness, and self-improvement within the Godly walk.

Philippians 2:3

Let nothing be done through strife or vainglory, but in lowliness of mind let each esteem others better than themselves.

Original Text:

What a terrible thing it is when one is compelled toward rivalry or excessive boasting with individuals in the faith, to gain attention. Such behavior is without the expectation of a believer.

Commentary:

In Philippians 2:3, the author emphasizes the importance of humility and warns against the destructive nature of pride. The desire to gain attention or compete with others in the faith can lead to a self-centered mindset that is contrary to the expectations of a believer. The focus should be on serving and loving others, rather than seeking personal recognition or glory.

Reflective Question:

Do you find yourself struggling with feelings of rivalry or the desire to boast excessively within your community of faith? How can you shift your focus from self-promotion to serving and loving others? In what ways can you practice humility in your relationships with others?

Original Text:

Self-examination begets honesty and honesty with one's own self builds self-confidence. This is a mystery. It is only when one can look from within and "know thy self", that one gains confidence. Where there is an absence of self-confidence there will be selfishness, and where there is selfishness there also, is self-centeredness. To this is added that a self-centered person reflects self-talk at its' worst extreme. This kind of self-talk negates the opportunity to share with others. When we share with one another, therein will be demonstrated either self-centeredness or the esteeming of others better than ourselves.

Commentary:

Self-examination is a critical component of personal growth and development. It enables us to better understand who we are, what we believe, and how we want to live our lives. When we examine ourselves honestly, we become more confident in our abilities and more comfortable in our own skin. This new-found confidence can be a powerful force for positive change in our lives and in the lives of those around us.

However, self-examination can also be a double-edged sword. When we focus too much on ourselves, we risk becoming self-centered and selfish, which can undermine our relationships with others. This is particularly true when we engage in negative self-talk, which can reinforce feelings of low self-esteem and make it more challenging to connect with others in a meaningful way. To avoid these pitfalls, it's essential to balance self-examination with a focus on others, seeking to understand and empathize with their perspectives while valuing our own.

Reflective Question:

How do you balance self-examination with a focus on others? In what ways do you build self-confidence while also demonstrating respect and compassion for those around you? How do you respond when you find yourself becoming too self-centered or negative in your self-talk?

Original Text:

It is not what we say to ourselves, but what others say about us that is the true measure of the inward self, presented outwardly. This outward presentation, where there is lowliness of mind or respectfulness toward others (love thy neighbor as thy self), allows one to reconcile his or her own former state with one's present state, and promote the better good in those that are in the faith.

Commentary:

This passage emphasizes the importance of how we present ourselves outwardly and how others perceive us. It suggests that the way we are seen by others is a reflection of our true selves and that our words and actions should demonstrate humility and respectfulness towards others. The author also emphasizes the need to reconcile our former selves with our present state, acknowledging that we are all works in progress and that we should strive to promote the better good in those around us.

Reflective Question:

How do you present yourself to others, and how do you think others perceive you? Are you mindful of your words and actions, and do they reflect humility and respectfulness towards others? How can you work towards reconciling your former self with your present state, and promote the better good in those around you?

Conclusion: Know Thy Self

In Philippians 2:3, we are reminded to avoid excessive boasting and rivalry within the faith and to instead practice lowliness of mind and esteem others better than ourselves. Self-examination and honesty with oneself are important for building self-confidence but must be balanced with a focus on others to avoid selfishness and self-centeredness. The way we present ourselves outwardly reflects our true selves, and we should strive to promote the better good in those around us. By knowing ourselves and practicing humility and respectfulness, we can deepen our relationships with others and grow in our Christian walk.

Chapter 19

A Life Promise

Amos 5:4

Our God is an awesome God, he reigns from heaven above and in his power and love, our god is an awesome God. This is the only God whom we call Father, not in the paternal pattern of an earthly father, but in the majesty of one who is an all-encompassing, all-consuming God of the universe. It is God to whom commanded his people to seek Him to live. This is a definite and never changing command and promise.

One has only to read a few verses of the Book of Amos to know the people of God were not seeking Him. Their hope and object of protection and concern were in areas where God did not exist. Israel had made allegiances and alliances that blurred their vision, and they seemed to have forgotten that God is their stronghold; a present help in the time of need.

There is nothing more that God has and continues to desire of His people today than that we seek Him first. Not opting to the left or the right. Not swearing upon things above or things below. Not given to false securities or shallow promises. Not even giving into devices that may have been confidences in the past, yet remain without actual power today.

It is this "Father" who is far superior than an earthly father and like an earthly father, wants only good things for his children. How then can a child have what the Father has for him/her least each seek His goodness? While children may adore the game of hide and seek, God is playing no game but rather, He is in a stationary place, open to all who would pierce the visible shroud of false confidences and behold His goodness.

Seek ye me and ye shall live... a hope for the day; a promise for the ages.

Introduction: A Life Promise

Amos 5:4 tells us that the Lord our God is an awesome God, commanding us to seek Him in order to truly live. This commandment remains unchanged and is just as relevant today as it was in biblical times. The Book of Amos shows us that God's people were not seeking Him as they should, and their allegiances and alliances were leading them astray. God desires only good things for His children and wants us to seek His goodness above all else.

In this chapter, we will explore the importance of seeking God in our daily lives, and how doing so can lead to a fulfilling and purposeful existence. Through the hope of this life promise, we will discover how seeking God is the key to unlocking a deeper understanding of His love and goodness.

Amos 5:4

For thus saith the Lord unto the house of Israel, Seek ye me, and ye shall live.

Original Text:

Our God is an awesome God, he reigns from heaven above and in his power and love, our god is an awesome God. This is the only God whom we call Father, not in the paternal pattern of an earthly father, but in the majesty of one who is an all-encompassing, all-consuming God of the universe. It is God who commanded his people to seek Him to live. This is a definite and never changing command and promise.

Commentary:

This passage highlights the majesty and power of God, who reigns over all creation from heaven above. The author emphasizes that God is not just a paternal figure in the traditional sense, but an all-encompassing, all-consuming God of the universe. The passage also points out that seeking God is a command that is never changing and one that is essential for true life.

Reflective Question:

What does it mean to you that God is an all-encompassing, all-consuming God of the universe? How do you approach seeking God in your daily life? Do you see it as a definite and never-changing command, or do you struggle with making it a priority? How can you make seeking God a more central part of your life?

Original Text:

One has only to read a few verses of the Book of Amos to know the people of God were not seeking Him. Their hope and object of protection and concern were in areas where God did not exist. Israel had made allegiances and alliances that blurred their vision, and they seemed to have forgotten that God is their stronghold; a present help in the time of need.

Commentary:

The Book of Amos is a prophetic message to the people of Israel, who had strayed far from God and were not seeking Him. Instead, they had placed their hope and trust in earthly alliances and false securities, which had clouded their vision and led them astray. Amos reminds them that God is their ultimate stronghold and source of protection and that they must turn back to Him in order to live.

Reflective Question:

How do we place our hope and trust in earthly things, rather than seeking God? How do these allegiances and alliances blur our vision and lead us away from God's will for our lives? What steps can we take to refocus our attention and seek God as our ultimate stronghold and source of protection?

Original Text:

There is nothing more that God has and continues to desire of His people today than that we seek Him first. Not opting to the left or the right. Not swearing upon things above or things below. Not given to false securities or shallow promises. Not even giving into devices that may have been confidences in the past, yet remain without actual power today.

Commentary:

God desires His people to seek Him first above all else. This means not being swayed by false securities or shallow promises, and not relying on devices or confidences that may have worked in the past but no longer hold power. God wants His people to have a genuine and deep relationship with Him, to seek Him wholeheartedly, and to make Him the center of their lives.

Reflective Question:

What false securities or shallow promises may distract you from seeking God? How can you prioritize seeking God in your life, and make Him the center of your thoughts and actions? In what ways can you deepen your relationship with God and seek Him wholeheartedly?

Original Text:

It is this "Father" who is far superior than an earthly father and like an earthly father, wants only good things for his children. How then can a child have what the Father has for him/her least each seek His goodness? While children may adore the game of hide and seek, God is playing no game but rather, He is in a stationary place, open to all who would pierce the visible shroud of false confidences and behold His goodness.

Commentary:

The comparison between God and an earthly father is often used in the Bible to illustrate God's love and care for His people. In this passage, the author emphasizes that God wants only good things for His children and that seeking His goodness is the key to receiving His blessings. The analogy of hide and seek is used to illustrate the idea that God is always present and ready to be found by those who seek Him. The use of the word "pierce" implies that breaking through the barriers that keep us from seeing God's goodness requires effort and persistence.

Reflective Question:

How do you view God's role as a father in your life? Do you believe that He wants only good things for you, or do you sometimes doubt His love and care? What are some ways that you can seek God's goodness and pierce through the barriers that keep you from experiencing His presence?

Original Text:
Seek ye me and ye shall live... a hope for the day; a promise for the ages.

Commentary:
This passage from the Book of Amos is a call to seek God above all else. It is a promise that those who seek Him will find life, both in this present moment and for eternity. The invitation to seek God is not only a command but also an opportunity to experience His goodness and faithfulness.

Reflective Question:
How often do you prioritize seeking God above all else in your daily life?

Conclusion: A Life Promise

The life promise presented in Amos 5:4 is a timeless reminder of the importance of seeking God. Through the Book of Amos, we are reminded of the dangers of placing our hope and trust in earthly things and the necessity of turning back to God as our ultimate source of strength and protection. Seeking God requires effort and persistence, but it is a promise for the ages and a hope for the day. By making God the center of our lives and seeking His goodness, we can experience a life of purpose and fulfillment, both now and for eternity.

Chapter 20

The Fear of God is Demonstrated Appreciation

Ecclesiastes 8:12

It shall be well with them that fear God. Notice the writer does not say it is well, but that it shall be well. This means that as one lives in the present so is his/her days numbered from the present into the future. To fear God is to love Him demonstrably as He views and observes one's lifestyle.

A lifestyle of love is far better than one that is absent love, and takes for granted the goodness of God. This is the state of sinfulness: one living on a dare in the presence of an all-knowing God. God knows the ignorance of those who do evil over and over again. This doing is out of ignorance and like a loving and long- suffering Father, God is patient and thereby, prolongs the days of the sinner; not wanting any to be lost or removed forever from His presence.

Fear before Him is an expression of who a person is and his/her awareness of the One who is greater. That God is greater does not give cause to tremble but to rejoice in knowing one's humility and in this humility, is acceptance that God is love and desires/offers the very best to those who fear Him.

Introduction: The Fear of God is Demonstrated Appreciation

Ecclesiastes 8:12 reminds us that those who fear God will experience a sense of well-being in their lives. However, this fear is not a fearful terror but rather a deep appreciation and reverence for the greatness of God. The writer highlights that this fear is not just a thought or feeling but is demonstrated through one's lifestyle and actions. Living a life of love and demonstrating appreciation towards God is far better than a life that takes His goodness for granted. Sinfulness is living without this appreciation and taking the presence of an all-knowing God for granted. Despite this, God's love is patient and merciful, desiring the best for all who fear Him.

In this chapter, we will explore the concept of the fear of God and how it is demonstrated through our lives, and how it leads to a deeper appreciation of His love and goodness.

Ecclesiastes 8:12

"Though a sinner do evil a hundred times, and his days be prolonged, yet surely I know that it shall be well with them that fear God, which fear before him:"

Original Text:

It shall be well with them that fear God. Notice the writer does not say it is well, but that it shall be well. This means that as one lives in the present so is his/her days numbered from the present into the future. To fear God is to love Him demonstrably as He views and observes one's lifestyle.

Commentary:

The writer of Ecclesiastes reminds us that those who fear God will be blessed and that it shall be well with them. The use of the future tense implies that blessings are yet to come and will be realized in the future. The writer also emphasizes that fearing God is not simply a matter of acknowledging His existence, but of loving Him and demonstrating this love through one's lifestyle. This is a reminder that true fear of God involves a deep reverence and respect for Him, and a desire to live according to His will.

Reflective Question:

What does it mean to you to fear God? How do you demonstrate this fear in your daily life? In what ways do you strive to live according to God's will and show your love for Him? Do you believe it will be well with those who fear God, even in difficult times?

Original Text:

A lifestyle of love is far better than one that is absent love, and takes for granted the goodness of God. This is the state of sinfulness: one living on a dare in the presence of an all knowing God. God knows the ignorance of those who do evil over and over again. This doing is out of ignorance and like a loving and long- suffering Father, God is patient and thereby, prolongs the days of the sinner; not wanting any to be lost or removed forever from His presence.

Commentary:

The author of this passage emphasizes the importance of living a life of love and appreciation for God, rather than taking His goodness for granted. The state of sinfulness is described as one of daring to live in the presence of an all-knowing God without regard for His will or the consequences of one's actions. However, God is described as a loving and patient Father who prolongs the days of sinners in the hopes that they will turn back to Him and not be lost forever. This passage emphasizes both the gravity of sin and the grace of God in extending patience and forgiveness.

Reflective Question:

How do you view God's patience and forgiveness toward sinners? Have you ever taken God's goodness for granted, and if so, how did you reconcile with Him? In what ways can you demonstrate appreciation for God in your daily life?

Original Text:

Fear before Him is an expression of who a person is and his/her awareness of the One who is greater. That God is greater does not give cause to tremble but to rejoice in knowing one's humility and in this humility is acceptance that God is love and desires/offers the very best to those who fear Him.

Commentary:

The fear of God is not simply about being afraid of His wrath or punishment, but it is also an expression of our awareness of God's greatness and our humility before Him. It is a recognition that we are not the center of the universe and that there is a greater power at work. When we fear God, we acknowledge His sovereignty and His love for us, which is demonstrated through

His desire to offer us the very best. Through this humility and acceptance, we can fully experience God's love and grace.

Reflective Question:

How do you understand the concept of "fearing God"? What does it mean to you to acknowledge God's greatness and your own humility in His presence? In what ways can you express your awareness of God's love for you through your fear of Him?

Conclusion: The Fear of God is Demonstrated Appreciation

The fear of God is not simply a matter of acknowledging His existence or being afraid of punishment. Rather, it is a deep appreciation and reverence for His greatness, which is demonstrated through our love and obedience to Him. Living a lifestyle of love and appreciation for God is far better than taking His goodness for granted, and it is through this humility and acceptance that we can fully experience His love and grace. As Ecclesiastes 8:12 reminds us, it shall be well with those who fear God, and through our fear of Him, we can find a deeper appreciation for His love and goodness in our lives.

Chapter 21

All Flesh Shall Worship Him Says the Lord

Isaiah 66:23

What an amazing plan! Every day, someone yields to the Lord as all flesh moves toward worship before the Lord.

Oftentimes the only reports heard from the media are those that accentuate crime, disorder, and/or a bad state of affairs, if only there would be reports about the good that is transpiring daily. Good things that make people take another look at what and how they are treating one another are what ought to be reported, unfortunately, it is the good things that are not reported; the things that bring a tear to the eye, a smile to the face, or a tingling within the soul. These are the things that should be reported for they make us say, "It is good".

Good things are a pronouncement of the love of God. Even He, with the unfolding of every day, spoke and continues to speak the immortal words, "It is good.'

On a daily basis people are actually coming to the Lord and worshipping before him. Some are people who once caused hurt, pain, and lots of tears. Some are innocent before God and never knew they were out of the ark of safety. Some are new believers. Some are mature individuals who looked at the goodness of God and in ignorance, scoffed and continued without concern nor care of consequences, but are now returning with a repented heart to worship Him. It is God's long suffering and His works within the life of mankind that provides this opportunity for people to come to Him on a daily basis.

When considering one new moon to another, this is a thirty-day cycle or one month's duration, likewise, when considering one Sabbath to another, this is the Hebrew equivalent of one week to the next, or Islam's one Jhuma to the next Jhuma. Notice in these measures it is one month to one week rather than the reverse. I perceive an adding of the cumulative as captured from the weekly count. How great thou art! Perhaps it is because the daily count is such that the weekly figures are best seen as a cumulative whole. Amazing! This is actually the budding of fruit; from one branch comes many new buds and from a clustered bud, lots of fruit.

Fruit, when it is ripe Is observed (worshipped) and when the observation is complete, the soul of the worshipper is refreshed and God is glorified. The glory of God through the span of time touches the heart of men and women, the effect is good, and the spark of love continues the cycle that draws flesh to worship before me, saith the Lord. Amazing is His plan!

Introduction: All Flesh shall Worship Him Says the Lord

The scripture in Isaiah 66:23 declares that all flesh shall worship the Lord. This is a remarkable promise that speaks to the power of God's love and grace to draw all people to Himself. Despite the negative reports that dominate media, there are daily occurrences of people yielding to the Lord and worshipping Him. This includes individuals who were once lost and causing harm, as well as new and mature believers. It is God's long-suffering and works in the lives of people that provide this opportunity for daily worship. The passage also highlights the importance of recognizing and reporting the good that is transpiring daily, as it is a pronouncement of God's love. The cycle of worship and the glory of God continues to touch the hearts of people and draw them closer to Him. In this chapter, we will explore the promise of all flesh worshipping the Lord and the impact of daily worship in our lives.

Isaiah 66:23:

And it shall come to pass, that from one new moon to another, and from one sabbath to another, shall all flesh come to worship before me, saith the LORD.

Original Text:

What an amazing plan! Every day, someone yields to the Lord as all flesh moves toward worship before the Lord.

Commentary:

This passage highlights the incredible plan of God, which is that every day someone will yield to Him and move towards worship. It emphasizes the ongoing nature of God's work in the world and the fact that people are constantly being drawn to Him. It also reminds us that every person has the opportunity to come to the Lord and worship Him, no matter their past or present circumstances.

Reflective Question:

How do you see God's plan unfolding in your life and in the world around you? Have you ever experienced a moment of yielding to the Lord and moving towards worship? In what ways can you be more open to God's work in your life and the lives of others?

Original Text:

Oftentimes the only reports heard from the media are those that accentuate crime, disorder, and/or a bad state of affairs, if only there would be reports about the good that is transpiring daily. Good things that make people take another look at what and how they are treating one another are what ought to be reported, unfortunately, it is the good things that are not reported; the things that bring a tear to the eye, a smile to the face, or a tingling within the soul. These are the things that should be reported for they make us say, "It is good".

Commentary:

The author of this passage laments the fact that media reports tend to focus on negative news, such as crime and disorder, rather than the good things that happen in the world on a daily basis. The author suggests that reporting on positive events and actions can inspire people to treat each other better and can have a positive impact on society. This passage reminds us that it is important to seek out and acknowledge the good in the world, even when it may not be readily apparent.

Reflective Question:
How do you feel about the media's focus on negative news? Do you think it has an impact on how people perceive the world? How do you try to seek out and appreciate the good things that happen in your life and in the world around you?

Original Text:
Good things are a pronouncement of the love of God. Even He, with the unfolding of every day, spoke and continues to speak the immortal words, "It is good.'

Commentary:
This passage reminds us that the goodness we experience in the world around us is a reflection of God's love for us. From the beauty of nature to the kindness of others, we can see God's love and care in everything that is good. The reference to God's words "It is good" recalls the account of creation in the book of Genesis, where God declares His creation to be good. This reminds us that God is the source of all that is good in the world and that His love for us is the reason for this goodness.

Reflective Question:
How do you recognize and appreciate the good things in your life as a reflection of God's love? In what ways can you share the goodness you experience with others to bring hope and joy to their lives?

Original Text:

On a daily basis people are actually coming to the Lord and worshipping before him. Some are people who once caused hurt, pain, and lots of tears. Some are innocent before God and never knew they were out of the ark of safety. Some are new believers. Some are mature individuals who looked at the goodness of God and in ignorance, scoffed and continued without concern nor care of consequences, but are now returning with a repented heart to worship Him. It is God's long suffering and His works within the life of mankind that provides this opportunity for people to come to Him on a daily basis.

Commentary:

This passage highlights the daily reality of people coming to the Lord and worshipping before Him, no matter their background or previous actions. The writer notes that some are individuals who have caused harm in the past, while others are innocent or new believers. Still, others are mature individuals who have come to recognize the goodness of God and have turned their hearts towards worship. The author attributes this opportunity to the long-suffering nature of God and His work in the lives of individuals.

Reflective Question:

How does the idea of God's long-suffering and patience in our lives inspire you to come to Him daily in worship? In what ways have you personally experienced God's grace and mercy in your life, and how has this impacted your relationship with Him? How can you extend the same grace and mercy to others who may be in need of God's love and forgiveness?

Original Text:

When considering one new moon to another, this is a thirty-day cycle or one month's duration, likewise, when considering one Sabbath to another, this is the Hebrew equivalent of one week to the next, or Islam's one Jhuma to the next Jhuma. Notice in these measures it is one month to one week rather than the reverse. I perceive an adding of the cumulative as captured from the weekly count. How great thou art! Perhaps it is because the daily count is such that the weekly figures are best seen as a cumulative whole. Amazing! This is actually the budding of fruit; from one branch comes many new buds and from a clustered bud, lots of fruit.

Commentary:

In this passage, the author reflects on the significance of measuring time in different cultures and religions. The focus is on the Hebrew calendar and the Sabbath, which is observed weekly, and the new moon, which occurs monthly. The author observes that there is a greater emphasis on the monthly cycle in the Hebrew calendar, whereas the weekly cycle is more prominent in Islam. The author reflects on the possibility that this is because the daily count is seen as a cumulative whole, and that the weekly count is a result of adding up the daily counts. This observation leads the author to marvel at the amazing plan of God, comparing it to the budding of fruit from a single branch.

Reflective Question:

What significance do you attach to the way time is measured in your culture or religion? How does the way you measure time reflect your values and beliefs? Do you believe there is a deeper meaning or purpose behind the way time is measured and observed?

Original Text:

Fruit, when it is ripe, it is observed (worshipped) and when the observation is complete, the soul of the worshipper is refreshed and God is glorified. The glory of God through the span of time touches the heart of men and women, the effect is good, and the spark of love continues the cycle that draws flesh to worship before me, saith the Lord. Amazing is His plan!

Commentary:

This passage emphasizes the importance of worshiping God and the beauty of the process of bearing fruit. The author compares the observation of ripe fruit to worship, suggesting that in the same way, we appreciate and celebrate the beauty and bounty of the natural world, we should appreciate and celebrate the glory of God. The author also suggests that this process of worshiping God and observing His works is cyclical, with the spark of love continuing to draw people towards worship and adoration.

Reflective Question:

How do you personally appreciate and celebrate the beauty and glory of God in your daily life? In what ways do you participate in the cyclical process of worship and adoration, and how does this process impact your spiritual life? How can you encourage others to participate in this process and draw them towards worshiping God?

Conclusion: All Flesh Shall Worship Him Says the Lord

The promise of all flesh worshipping the Lord is an incredible plan that speaks to the power of God's love and grace to draw all people to Himself. The passage encourages us to seek out and appreciate the good in the world, recognizing that it is a pronouncement of God's love. We are also reminded of the daily reality of people coming to the Lord and worshipping Him, no matter their background or previous actions. The significance of measuring time and the importance of worshiping God are also emphasized. Overall, this chapter invites us to reflect on the impact of daily worship in our lives and the amazing plan of God to draw all flesh to Himself.

Chapter 22

Keep the Word
of God

Deuteronomy 11:18

The word of God is especially important, and we are commanded to keep His word in our heart, soul, and hand; to hold (keep) It in sight (mind) as we venture life. There are corresponding verses that likewise emphasize the need to keep the word of God.

Keeping the word of God means to read, meditate, study, and actualize its' application every day. To neglect to do so parallels eating good food and not appreciating the varying tastes, or looking in the mirror and failing to notice the changes occurring in one's physical form, or perhaps being injured and not noticing the loss of blood, sensation or use of the injured part.

This Bible verse supposes the first rule: that of knowing God's word. It is the "therefore "that alludes to a previous action and leans toward a continued activity; the former being required if the latter is to be accomplished.

Thus, for one to know the word of God there is the requisite for us to make the word a priority in human growth and development. So, when parents or guardians fail to present the Word, children are absent the initial and necessary introduction to "lay up these my words ", until Grace introduces the content of the Word in alternate settings. It is the alternate settings that leave even the most remote of life circumstances without excuse. As God has commanded, so He will avail "settings" for all to be exposed to His Word.

The beautiful part is, the sooner one is exposed to the Word, the more likely will be the practice to "lay up these my words in your heart and in your soul, and bind them for a sign upon your hand; a sign that will be visible to the 'keeper' through application, and to the world for example.

When the Word becomes "as frontlets between your eyes", the mark of adoption is more spiritual. Like the forehead of certain birds, the frontlet has a different color from the rest of the head. This color is exemplified in one's outwardly consistent behavior, manner, approach, appetites, etc. Thus, one who has the Word will be different from the world and this difference will directly correspond with the ingesting of the Word on a continuous basis.

Therefore, and finally, what is from and is received of God becomes like God. This is the answer to why God commands us to be mindful of His word; a Word needing presentation as early and as often as possible.

Introduction: Keep the Word of God

In the book of Deuteronomy, we are commanded to keep the word of God in our heart, soul, and hand, and to hold it in sight as we navigate through life. Keeping the word of God is not just about reading it, but also about meditating, studying, and applying it in our daily lives. In this way, the word of God becomes a part of us and shapes our behavior, approach, and attitudes. It is essential that we prioritize the word of God in our growth and development, starting with its presentation in childhood. This ensures that we develop a deep understanding and appreciation for the word of God, and its application becomes second nature to us. As we keep the word of God, we become more like Him and exemplify His glory to the world. So let us be mindful of His word and make it a priority in our lives, for in doing so, we become more like God.

Deuteronomy 11:18:

Therefore, shall ye lay up these my words in your heart and in your soul, and bind them for a sign upon your hand, that they may be as frontlets between your eyes.

Original Text:

The word of God is especially important, and we are commanded to keep His word in our heart, soul, and hand; to hold (keep) It in sight (mind) as we venture (live) life. There are corresponding verses that likewise emphasize the need to keep the word of God.

Commentary:

The writer emphasizes the importance of the Word of God and the commandment to keep it in our hearts, souls, and hands. The passage emphasizes that the Word of God is not just something to be read and studied, but something that needs to be integrated into every aspect of our lives. The reference to corresponding verses suggests that this commandment is not just a one-time instruction, but a theme that is repeated throughout scripture.

Reflective Question:

How do you prioritize the Word of God in your daily life? In what ways do you integrate the teachings of the Bible into your thoughts, actions, and decisions? How do you ensure that you are keeping the Word of God in sight as you venture through life?

Original Text:

Keeping the word of God means to read, meditate, study, and actualize its' application every day. To neglect to do so parallels eating good food and not appreciating the varying tastes, or looking in the mirror and failing to notice the changes occurring in one's physical form, or perhaps being injured and not noticing the loss of blood, sensation or use of the injured part.

Commentary:

This passage emphasizes the importance of actively engaging with the word of God in order to fully appreciate its value and transformative power. The metaphor of food and taste suggests that just as we can savor and appreciate the different flavors of good food, we can also savor and appreciate the richness of God's word by regularly engaging with it through reading, meditation, study, and application. The analogy of the mirror and physical form highlights the importance of self-reflection and self-awareness in our spiritual lives, as neglecting to notice changes or injuries can have serious consequences. In the same way, neglecting to engage with God's word can lead to spiritual stagnation or even harm.

Reflective Question:

How do you actively engage with the word of God in your daily life? In what ways do you make time for reading, meditation, study, and application of the Bible's teachings? How has this practice impacted your spiritual growth and awareness? In what ways can you encourage others to develop a similar practice of engaging with the word of God?

Original Text:

This Bible verse supposes the first rule: that of knowing God's word. It is the "therefore "that alludes to a previous action and leans toward a continued activity; the former being required if the latter is to be accomplished.

Commentary:

This passage emphasizes the importance of knowing God's word as the first rule in keeping it. The use of the word "therefore" implies that there is a previous action or knowledge that is necessary to continue the activity of keeping God's word. This suggests that knowing and understanding God's word is a foundational step in being able to live it out and apply it in our daily lives.

Reflective Question:

How important is it to you to have a deep understanding of God's word? In what ways do you actively seek to increase your knowledge and understanding of the Bible? How has this knowledge impacted your ability to live out God's word in your daily life?

Original Text:

Thus, for one to know the word of God there is the requisite for us to make the word a priority in human growth and development. So, when parents or guardians fail to present the Word, children are absent the initial and necessary introduction to "lay up these my words ", until Grace introduces the content of the Word in alternate settings. It is the alternate settings that leave even the most remote of life circumstances without excuse. As God has commanded, so He will avail "settings" for all to be exposed to His Word.

Commentary:

This passage emphasizes the importance of introducing children to the word of God at an early age. The author suggests that parents and guardians have a responsibility to present the Word to their children and to make it a priority in their growth and development. This is because knowing the Word of God is crucial for spiritual growth and development, and neglecting to do so can result in children being without the initial and necessary introduction to the Word.

However, the author notes that even if parents or guardians fail to present the Word, there are alternate settings in which individuals can be exposed to the Word. These alternate settings leave even the most remote of life circumstances without excuse, as God will make sure that opportunities to encounter His Word are provided.

The passage highlights the idea that exposure to the Word of God is essential for spiritual growth and development. It emphasizes the responsibility of parents and guardians to introduce children to the Word, but also recognizes that individuals can encounter the Word in other settings as well. It underscores the importance of making the Word of God a priority in one's life, and the responsibility that comes with being exposed to it.

Reflective Question:

How has exposure to the Word of God impacted your spiritual growth and development? Do you feel that you were introduced to the Word at an early age? If not, how did you encounter the Word later in life? How can you make the Word of God a priority in your daily life, and what responsibility do you feel comes with being exposed to it?

Original Text:

The beautiful part is, the sooner one is exposed to the Word, the more likely will be the practice to "lay up these my words in your heart and in your soul, and bind them for a sign upon your hand"; a sign that will be visible to the 'keeper' through application, and to the world for example.

Commentary:

In this passage, the author emphasizes the importance of being exposed to the Word of God at an early age. The earlier one is introduced to the Word, the more likely they are to make it a part of their daily practice and internalize its teachings. The author notes that this practice of laying up the Word in one's heart and soul and binding it as a sign upon their hand will be visible to both the individual and the world.

This passage highlights the impact of early exposure to the Word of God in shaping an individual's beliefs, values, and behavior. It suggests that the Word of God can serve as a moral compass, guiding individuals in their daily decisions and actions. The author notes that the Word of God can serve as a visible sign to the world of an individual's faith and commitment to following God's teachings.

Reflective Question:

How has your exposure to the Word of God impacted your beliefs and values? In what ways has it influenced your behavior and decision-making? How do you make the Word a priority in your daily life and ensure that you are internalizing its teachings? How can you make the Word a more visible sign of your faith in the world around you?

Original Text:

When the Word becomes "as frontlets between your eyes", the mark of adoption is more spiritual. Like the forehead of certain birds, the frontlet has a different color from the rest of the head. This color is exemplified in one's outwardly consistent behavior, manner, approach, appetites, etc. Thus, one who has the Word will be different from the world and this difference will directly correspond with the ingesting of the Word on a continuous basis.

Commentary:

In this passage, the author uses a metaphor of a frontlet to describe the spiritual impact of keeping the Word of God in one's heart and soul. The frontlet, which is a decorative band worn on the forehead of certain birds, stands out from the rest of the head and signifies a distinction. The author suggests that the Word of God should be so ingrained in a person's heart and soul that it becomes like a frontlet between their eyes, signifying a spiritual difference that sets them apart from the world. This difference is exemplified through consistent outward behavior, approach, and appetites, which reflect a transformed and renewed mind.

The author's use of the metaphor highlights the importance of the Word of God in transforming a person's life and character. The more a person ingests the Word of God on a continuous basis, the more it will transform their thoughts, feelings, and actions, making them more Christ-like. This transformation will be visible to others, and likewise, they will recognize the difference in the person's behavior and attitudes.

The passage also suggests that keeping the Word of God should be a continuous and ongoing process. It should not be a one-time event or a sporadic activity, but rather a daily habit that is incorporated into one's life. This ongoing practice of keeping the Word of God in one's heart and soul will lead to a spiritual difference that sets one apart from the world.

Reflective Question:

How can you make keeping the Word of God a daily habit in your life? In what ways do you see the Word of God transforming your thoughts, feelings, and actions? How can you ensure that this transformation is visible to others, reflecting the distinction that comes from keeping the Word of God in your heart and soul?

Original Text:

Therefore, and finally, what is from and is received of God becomes like God. This is the answer to why God commands us to be mindful of His word; a Word needing presentation as early and as often as possible.

Commentary:

In this final statement, the author emphasizes the transformative power of God's word. The idea that what is received from God becomes like God is not only a reflection of the nature of God but also a call to action for believers. The author suggests that the continuous ingestion of God's word is necessary for believers to become more like God.

This idea is supported by other biblical passages that speak of the transformative power of God's word. In Romans 12:2, believers are instructed to be transformed by the renewing of their minds, which can be accomplished through the study and application of God's word. Similarly, in 2 Corinthians 3:18, it is stated that as believers behold the glory of the Lord, they are transformed into His image.

The author's call to be mindful of God's word and to present it as early and as often as possible speaks to the importance of nurturing one's faith and spiritual growth. It highlights the role of parents, guardians, and communities in ensuring that children and new believers have access to the word of God, and in helping them to develop a deep and meaningful relationship with Him.

Reflective Question:

How has the word of God transformed your life? In what ways have you seen the transformative power of God's word at work in your own behavior, thoughts, and attitudes? What steps can you take to be more mindful of God's word and to present it to others as early and as often as possible?

Conclusion: Keep the Word of God

This chapter emphasized the importance of keeping the word of God in our hearts, souls, and hands. It is not enough to simply read the Bible; we must actively engage with it through reading, meditation, study, and application. The earlier one is introduced to the Word, the more likely they are to make it a part of their daily practice and internalize its teachings. Keeping the Word of God in sight as we venture through life will guide our behavior, approach, and attitudes, and make us more like God. The Word of God has transformative power, and it is crucial to make it a priority in our growth and development. As believers, we have a responsibility to nurture our faith and spiritual growth, as well as to present the Word of God to others. How do we make the Word of God a priority in our daily lives, and how can we ensure that others have access to it? What steps can we take to actively engage with the Word of God and allow it to transform us from the inside out?

Chapter 23

An Instrument of His Pleasure; His Peace

Matthew 23:9

Oftentimes people place individuals, who "shoulder" them through situations upon pedestals as though these individuals are the supplier of disbursement in times of need. By doing so, the action becomes objectionable to God and the application is against His principle of looking to Him for all that is needed and is to be provided. The command to call no man Father addresses this objectionable application and practice, for he who provides must also be supplied, to provide.

God is the creator of the heavenly storehouse and He alone blesses and uses people to store up and release blessings. Where God uses people to bless, they are a mere instrument and ought not be revered but rather, are to be "thanked, blessed, and prayed for often", that they might remain an instrument of His pleasure and His peace.

At first, children know nothing save the nurturing-care of a mother and the provision-protection of a father. To these individuals are given the honorable recognition of mother and a father; collectively these are our parents. Soon, however, and as the word of God is given light into the lives of children, they learn that parents can only have and extend what the Father of heaven has caringly and deliberately given. They learn that He is both the nurturing Mother and the protecting Father who, like good parents, provides good things to His children.

Therefore, to call no man father upon the earth is not a prohibition against the title, but its application where reverence is exhausted toward one who has not authority within the heavenly storehouse. Whether one learns this principle early in life, during life or late in life the reality remains the same; that the all that one has belongs to God and He alone dispenses and disperses daily provision upon the earth, from the heavenly storehouse.

Introduction: An Instrument of His Pleasure, His Peace

In Matthew 23:9, Jesus commands His followers to call no man father upon the earth, but instead to look to God as the ultimate source of provision and blessing. This passage speaks to the danger of placing individuals on pedestals and revering them as the supplier of all our needs, rather than recognizing God as the ultimate provider.

The passage emphasizes that God alone is the creator of the heavenly storehouse, and He blesses and uses people as instruments to store up and release blessings. These individuals should not be revered, but rather thanked, blessed, and prayed for, that they may remain an instrument of God's pleasure and peace.

The passage highlights the importance of recognizing that all that we have belongs to God, and He alone dispenses and disperses daily provision upon the earth from the heavenly storehouse. As children grow and learn, they come to understand that parents can only have and extend what the Father of heaven has deliberately given.

In this chapter, we will explore the meaning and implications of Jesus' command to call no man father upon the earth. We will examine the principle of looking to God as the ultimate source of provision and blessing, and the dangers of placing individuals on pedestals. We will also explore the role of parents and guardians in nurturing children's faith and developing an understanding of God's provisions, and how we can all strive to be instruments of His pleasure and peace.

Matthew 23:9

And call no man your father upon the earth: for one is your Father, which is in heaven.

Original Text:

Oftentimes people place individuals, who "shoulder" them through situations upon pedestals as though these individuals are the supplier of disbursement in times of need. By doing so, the action becomes objectionable to God and the application is against His principle of looking to Him for all that is needed and is to be provided. The command to call no man Father addresses this objectionable application and practice, for he who provides must also be supplied, to provide.

Commentary:

This passage highlights the tendency of people to elevate other individuals to the status of a "savior" in their lives, attributing to them the power to provide for all their needs. This attitude is contrary to the principle of looking to God as the ultimate source of provision and blessing. When we put our faith in human beings, we limit ourselves to their abilities, which are finite and limited. We may even begin to idolize them, attributing to them qualities that only God possesses, such as omniscience, omnipotence, and omnipresence.

The command to call no man father is not a prohibition against recognizing the role of parents and guardians in our lives. Rather, it is a warning against giving them undue reverence and placing them on a pedestal as if they were the ultimate source of our well-being. By doing so, we disregard the fact that all good things come from God and that He alone is the source of all provision and blessing.

Reflective Question:

Do I place too much trust and reverence in people to provide for my needs, or do I look to God as the ultimate source of my provision and blessing? How can I cultivate a deeper trust in God's provision and learn to recognize His hand in my life?

Original Text

God is the creator of the heavenly storehouse and He alone blesses and uses people to store up and release blessings. Where God uses people to bless, they are a mere instrument and ought not be revered but rather, are to be "thanked, blessed, and prayed for often", that they might remain an instrument of His pleasure and His peace.

Commentary:

This statement highlights an important theological concept in acknowledging the sovereignty of God. God is the ultimate source of blessings, and it is He who chooses to bless people and use them as instruments to bless others. This underscores the fact that human beings are not the ultimate providers of anything, and should not be revered as such. Rather, they are merely instruments in the hands of God.

This concept has implications for how we view and treat others. When someone does something good for us or blesses us in some way, we should not view them as the ultimate source of that blessing but rather, acknowledge that God used them as an instrument to bless us. This perspective helps to guard against idolizing people and helps us to maintain a proper perspective on our relationship with God.

Additionally, the statement encourages us to express gratitude to those who have blessed us, while recognizing that it is God who ultimately deserves our thanks and praise. We should thank and bless people for their acts of kindness while praying that God would continue to use them as instruments of His pleasure and peace.

Reflective Question:

How can we cultivate a perspective of gratitude and recognition of God's sovereignty in our relationships with others, particularly those who have blessed us in some way?

Original Text:

At first, children know nothing save the nurturing-care of a mother and the provision-protection of a father. To these individuals are given the honorable recognition of mother and a father; collectively these are our parents. Soon, however, and as the word of God is given light into the lives of children, they learn that parents can only have and extend what the Father of heaven has caringly and deliberately given. They learn that He is both the nurturing Mother and the protecting Father who, like good parents, provides good things to His children.

Commentary:

This passage emphasizes the importance of recognizing God's role as the ultimate provider and caregiver, even in the context of earthly parents. While parents are given honorable recognition for their nurturing and protective care of their children, this passage reminds us that they are ultimately only able to provide and extend what God has already given.

As children grow and mature in their understanding of God's provision, they come to recognize that He is both a nurturing mother and a protecting father, who provides good things to His children. This recognition can help children develop a deeper faith and trust in God as their ultimate provider, even as they continue to honor and respect their earthly parents.

Reflective Question:

How can we help children develop a deeper understanding of God's provision and care, even in the context of their relationship with their earthly parents?

Original Text:

Therefore, to call no man father upon the earth is not a prohibition against the title but its application where reverence is exhausted toward one who has not authority within the heavenly storehouse. Whether one learns this principle early in life, during life or late in life the reality remains the same; that the all that one has belongs to God and He alone dispenses and disperses daily provision upon the earth, from the heavenly storehouse.

Commentary:

This passage emphasizes that the commandment to call no man father upon the earth is not a prohibition against the title itself, but rather against its improper application. The problem is not with the title, but with the way it is used when reverence is exhausted toward someone who does not have authority within the heavenly storehouse. This suggests that there is a distinction between earthly authority and heavenly authority and that the latter is the ultimate source of power and provision.

The passage also highlights the fact that everything that one has belongs to God, and that He alone is the one who dispenses and disperses daily provision upon the earth from the heavenly storehouse. This reinforces the idea that God is the ultimate source of power and provision, and that we should look to Him for all of our needs.

Reflective Question:

How can we ensure that we do not exhaust reverence towards someone who does not have authority within the heavenly storehouse?

Conclusion: An Instrument of His Pleasure, His Peace

In this chapter, we have explored the meaning and implications of Jesus' command to call no man father upon the earth. We have learned that the commandment is not a prohibition against recognizing the role of parents and guardians in our lives, but rather a warning against giving them undue reverence and placing them on a pedestal as if they were the ultimate source of our well-being. We have also learned that God is the ultimate source of provision and blessing, and that human beings are merely instruments in His hands. Therefore, we should thank, bless, and pray for those who have blessed us, recognizing that it is God who ultimately deserves our thanks and praise.

Furthermore, we have explored the importance of recognizing God's role as the ultimate provider and caregiver, even in the context of earthly parents. As children grow and mature in their understanding of God's provision, they come to recognize that He is both a nurturing mother and a protecting father, who provides good things to His children. This recognition can help children develop a deeper faith and trust in God as their ultimate provider, even as they continue to honor and respect their earthly parents.

Ultimately, the commandment to call no man father upon the earth reminds us that everything that we have belongs to God, and that He alone dispenses and disperses daily provision upon the earth from the heavenly storehouse. As we cultivate a deeper trust in God's provision, may we also seek to be instruments of His pleasure and peace, blessing others as He blesses us.

Chapter 24

Arise Shine for the Light is Come

Isaiah 60:1

This verse met me at a time when I needed an encouraging Word. It was a time when I had seemingly held my breath waiting for the manifestation of a daily prayer request. I was in what is characteristically described as an alley experience, where there is a need to behold the mountain top.

It is a climbing experience of faith. It is an experience that moves the very soul of one's being and makes one trust God or turn toward idols for provision. It is an experience that requires a trust in Him and Him alone for the entire journey. It is a time where focus is given toward a return to an era long given up for the sake of family and the hope of return as God deems well with or for me.

I have chosen to trust in Him who has and knows all things, believing the circumstances are directly linked to where God is taking me in the next and perhaps final chapter of my working life. I have no fear nor am I afraid, for I am resolved not to wait until the moment death is upon me before I give cause to totally entrust my state to God. He is and shall remain my strength, and it is He alone whom I trust.

Nevertheless, since coming to this time, there have been days of sadness, days of concern, days of wondering, so many days of longing for this time to be over, for the journey to be completed. Then the dayspring of life comes before me in the presence of this Bible verse. "Get up with joy!". It shouts, and knows that the end of the time is here! God has answered your prayer and the response is to rejoice!

Now faith is the substance of things hoped for, the evidence of things not seen. I have not seen the fullness of the time but I have been assured, this day that the end is placed, hopefully as I've asked, although certainly for my good.

Hallelujah!!!

Introduction: Arise Shine for the Light is Come

The verse "Arise, shine; for your light has come, and the glory of the Lord has risen upon you" is a powerful and encouraging message that speaks to the depths of our souls. It comes at a time when we need an encouraging word, when we find ourselves in a dark and difficult season, and we long for the light of God's presence to shine upon us.

In the midst of life's challenges, we often find ourselves in a valley experience, where we feel stuck and unable to see a way out. It is during these times that we must trust in God and Him alone for the journey ahead. We must cling to His promises and know that His plan for our lives is good.

This chapter is a reflection on the journey of faith, and the challenges and joys that come with it. It is a reminder that no matter what we face in life, we can always trust in God's faithfulness and love. We can rise up with joy and know that the end of the time of trial is here. God has answered our prayers and the response is to rejoice!

As we explore the message of Isaiah 60:1, may we be reminded that God's light shines upon us and that we are called to arise and shine with joy, knowing that He is faithful to bring us through every trial and challenge that we face.

Isaiah 60:1

Arise, shine; for your light has come, and the glory of the Lord has risen upon you

Original Text:

This verse met me at a time when I needed an encouraging Word. It was a time when I had seemingly held my breath waiting for the manifestation of a daily prayer request. I was in what is characteristically described as an alley experience, where there is a need to behold the mountain top.

Commentary:

This passage describes a personal experience of waiting for a prayer request to be answered. The author was in a difficult situation and was waiting for a breakthrough or a positive change. The author describes this as an "alley experience," which suggests that they were in a dark and difficult place, without a clear path forward. This may be a metaphorical description of a challenging time in the author's life, such as a period of uncertainty or crisis.

The author's experience of waiting for a prayer request to be answered is something that many people can relate. We often pray for things that we desperately want or need, but we do not always see immediate results. This can be frustrating, discouraging, and can even cause us to question our faith.

However, this passage also highlights the importance of hope and encouragement during difficult times. The author found solace in this Bible verse, which proved a reminder that there is light at the end of the tunnel. This suggests that the author had faith, the prayer would eventually be answered, and she would find relief from the current situation.

Reflective Question:

Have you ever been in a situation where you were waiting for a prayer request to be answered? How did you handle the waiting period, and what gave you hope and encouragement during that time?

Original Text:

It is a climbing experience of faith. It is an experience that moves the very soul of one's being and makes one trust God or turn toward idols for provision. It is an experience that requires a trust in Him and Him alone for the entire journey. It is a time where focus is given toward a return to an era long given up for the sake of family and the hope of return as God deems well with or for me.

Commentary:

This passage speaks to the experience of undergoing a challenging and faith-stretching journey in life. The author describes it as a climbing experience of faith, one that moves the very soul and requires complete trust in God for the entire journey. The journey can be so challenging that one may even consider turning towards idols for provision instead of trusting in God alone.

The passage highlights the importance of trusting God during difficult times, even when it seems easier to turn to other sources of support. It speaks to the need for perseverance and the willingness to let go of the past and embrace new possibilities that God may have in store. The author acknowledges that it can be difficult to give up the comfort of a familiar era or season, but reminds us that our hope should be in God's plan for our lives.

Reflective Question:

Have you ever gone through a challenging journey that required complete trust in God? How did you navigate that journey, and what did you learn about yourself and about God during that time?

Original Text:

I have chosen to trust in Him who has and knows all things, believing the circumstances are directly linked to where God is taking me in the next and perhaps final chapter of my working life. I have no fear nor am I afraid, for I am resolved not to wait until the moment death is upon me before I give cause to totally entrust my state to God. He is and shall remain my strength, and it is He alone whom I trust.

Commentary:

This statement is a powerful expression of faith and trust in God, even in the midst of difficult circumstances. The author acknowledges that the current situation may be linked to God's plan for the future, and thus, have made a deliberate choice to trust in Him for strength, perseverance and provisions. The author also emphasizes that this trust is not conditional to a certain outcome or a specific time frame but rather, a lifelong commitment to entrust her life to God.

This statement highlights the importance of trusting God throughout all stages of life, not just in times of crisis or uncertainty. It is a reminder that our trust in God should not be dependent on our circumstances or our own abilities, but rather on the unchanging ways of God who knows and controls all things.

The author's resolve to trust in God even in the final chapter of her working life is a powerful testimony to the transformative power of faith. It challenges readers to reflect on their own level of trust in God and encourages them to make a deliberate choice to entrust their lives to Him, regardless of their current circumstances.

Reflective Question:

How can we cultivate a deeper level of trust in God, even in the midst of difficult circumstances or uncertainty about the future? What steps can we take to ensure that our trust in God is not conditional on a specific outcome or time frame, but rather a lifelong commitment to entrust our life to Him?

Original Text:

Nevertheless, since coming to this time, there have been days of sadness, days of concern, days of wondering, so many days of longing for this time to be over, for the journey to be completed. Then the dayspring of life comes before me in the presence of this Bible verse. "Get up with joy!" it shouts, and know that the end of the time is here! God has answered your prayer and the response is to rejoice!

Commentary:

This passage captures the ups and downs of a journey of faith. The author acknowledges that despite their trust in God and His plan for their life, there have been difficult days filled with sadness, concern, and longing for the end of the journey. However, the author then describes a moment of clarity and hope, when a Bible verse speaks directly to them, providing encouragement and motivation to keep going.

This experience highlights the importance of being open to the ways in which God speaks to us, whether through scripture, prayer, or other means. It also reminds us that even in the midst of difficult times, there is always the possibility for a breakthrough, a moment of clarity or insight that can give us the strength and courage to keep moving forward.

The passage also emphasizes the importance of rejoicing when God answers our prayers, even if the answer is not exactly what we had hoped for or expected. It is a reminder that God's plan for our lives is always greater than our own, and that even in the midst of difficulties, He is working to bring about His purposes.

Reflective Question:

How can we remain open to the ways in which God speaks to us, even in the midst of difficult times? How can we cultivate a spirit of rejoicing and gratitude when God answers our prayers, even if the answer is not what we had hoped for or expected?

Original Text:

Now faith is the substance of things hoped for, the evidence of things not seen. I have not seen the fullness of the time but I have been assured, this day that the end is placed, hopefully as I've asked, although certainly for my good. Hallelujah!!!

Commentary:

The statement "Now faith is the substance of things hoped for, the evidence of things not seen" is a powerful declaration about the nature of faith. It suggests that faith is not merely a feeling or a hope, but rather a substance; something that has tangible and real effects in our lives. Faith is not just a vague belief in something, but rather an assurance of things that we have yet to see.

The writer notes that they have not yet seen the fullness of the time, but they have been assured that the end is placed, hopefully as they have asked. This suggests a deep trust in God's provision and plan, even in the face of uncertainty and difficulty. The writer's faith has allowed her to hold onto hope, even when circumstances may have seemed bleak or uncertain.

The declaration of "Hallelujah!!!" is a fitting response to this understanding of faith. It is a joyful recognition of God's provision and goodness, even in the midst of challenging times. It is a reminder that no matter what we may face in life, we can always turn to God in faith and trust that He will guide us through.

Reflective Question:

How can we cultivate a deeper understanding of faith as a substance, rather than just a feeling or a hope? How can we learn to trust in God's provision and plan, even when we may not yet see the fullness of the time?

Conclusion: Arise Shine for the Light is Come

The message of Isaiah 60:1 is a powerful reminder of God's faithfulness and love, even in the midst of our darkest moments. This chapter has explored the experiences of a personal journey of faith, the challenges that come with it, and the importance of trusting in God throughout all stages of life. It has encouraged us to remain open to the ways in which God speaks to us, to cultivate a spirit of rejoicing and gratitude when He answers our prayers, and to deepen our understanding of faith as a substance. May we always remember that God's light shines upon us, and that we are called to arise and shine with joy, knowing that He is faithful to bring us through every trial and challenge that we face. Hallelujah!

Chapter 25

Do No Harm to Self
or Others

Genesis 22:7

Does God require the ultimate sacrifice: to give up one's life.

This is the lingering question in days of terrorist attacks and kamikaze raids. It is a day where innocent and unsuspecting people fall victim to the distorted concept that the ultimate honor to the "Almighty" is to die; this as an expression of God's rage against an injustice within the social fiber of humanity.

God has not made life to be a vanishing vapor at one's own hand. Human life's (as are other forms of life) are precious to God, for in man's being is the breath of God. Although Earth produces the substance necessary to clothe the inner parts, the outer clothing is useless where there is the absence of Holy breath. The Scriptures indicate that as a result of mankind receiving this breath, he/she became a living soul.

To live is to do that which is approved of Almighty God. It is too easy for God to remove his breath. We then, need not seek to remove it our self. So, it is with this scripture and another:

"O my lord! Grant me a righteous son. So, we gave him the good news of a boy (Isma'ili) ready to suffer and forebear. Then, when (the son) reached the age of serious work with him, he said: "O my son! I see in vision that I offer thee in sacrifice: Now see what is thy view! The son said: "O my father! Do as thou art commanded: Thou wilt find me, if Allah so wills one practicing patience and constancy! So, when they had both submitted their wills to Allah and he had laid him prostrate on his forehead for sacrifice, we called out to him, "O Abraham! Thou host already fulfilled the vision!". Thus, indeed do we reward those who do right. For this was obviously a trial - and we ransomed him with a momentous sacrifice, and we left this blessing for him among generations to come in later times. "Peace and Salutation to Abraham!" This indeed do We reward those who do right: for he was one of our believing Servants. And We gave him the good news of Isaac, a prophet: One of the Righteous. We blessed him and Isaac: but of their progeny are some that do right, and some

that obviously do wrong, to their own souls. The Holy Qur'an, Surah 37:100-113.

While both father and son went up to Mount Moriah to present a sacrifice, the boy, Isaac, was correct to question his father, Abraham, about the absence of what would be the sacrifice.

Often time in depictions of this scriptural scene, Abraham is seen grasping the tool of sacrifice in a position to do harm to the boy. To read the aligning and subsequent scriptures is to understand the action occurring prior to the Angel's call to Abraham. Genesis 22:10 states: And Abraham stretched forth his hand and took the knife to slay his son. As one is bringing his/her hand toward an object, is the action taking place? Abraham's hand only grasped the knife and his hand stayed in that position; upon his hearing the Angel speak. Abraham, then, was prohibited from even a threatening gesture of a raised knife over his son but rather, the distractions prevailed, and the true object of sacrifice revealed: a "prepared" ram caught in the thicket.

Even so and while not spared the agony of the journey to Mount Moriah, the development and arrangement of the altar, and the placement of Isaac thereupon, Abraham's obedience was tested only to the point of "preparing" or "displaying" Isaac as a sacrifice, rather than making or causing him to be the sacrifice. In other words, God's provision was implied in how he directed Abraham: to "offer" rather than "make" Isaac a sacrifice.

Therefore, and as God manifested the essence of his love toward both Abraham and Isaac in this scriptural depiction and by what was spoken prior to (offer of a sacrifice) and while upon Mount Moriah, "do the child no harm" either to ones' self or toward others.

Introduction: Do No Harm to Self or Others

The concept of sacrifice is a recurring theme in many religions, and it has been distorted and misused in various ways throughout history. In this chapter, the author explores the question of whether God requires the ultimate sacrifice of giving up one's life. This question has become particularly relevant in the context of terrorist attacks and kamikaze raids, where individuals believe that dying in the name of God is the ultimate honor.

The author looks to Genesis 22:7, which raises the question of whether God requires the ultimate sacrifice. The author argues that human life is precious to God, and that to live is to do what is approved of by God. The Scriptures indicate that God has given humans the breath of life, and that it is not for humans to take it away. The author uses the example of Abraham and Isaac to illustrate the importance of obedience to God's commands, and the need to do no harm to one's self or to others.

This chapter challenges readers to reflect on the true meaning of sacrifice, and to consider how their actions impact themselves and others. It is a reminder that God values human life and that our actions should reflect that value. Through the story of Abraham and Isaac, the author reminds us that obedience to God's commands is essential, and that we should always seek to do what is right in the eyes of God.

Genesis 22:7

And Isaac spake unto Abraham his father, and said, my father, and he said, here am I, my son. And he said, Behold the fire and the wood: but where is the lamb for a burnt offering?

Original Text:
Does God require the ultimate sacrifice: to give up one's life?

Commentary:
The question of whether God requires the ultimate sacrifice of giving up one's life has been a topic of debate for centuries. Some religious traditions hold that martyrdom is a noble act of faith and obedience, while others believe that preserving life is the ultimate goal of human existence. The idea of martyrdom as a form of divine sacrifice is often associated with extremist and violent interpretations of religious texts, and has been used to justify acts of terrorism and violence in the name of God.

The concept of sacrifice has deep roots in many religious traditions, including Judaism, Christianity, and Islam. In the Old Testament, we see numerous examples of animal sacrifices offered to God as a way of atoning for sin or expressing gratitude for blessings received. However, the ultimate sacrifice was not the life of an animal, but the life of God's own son, Jesus Christ, who died on the cross for the sins of humanity.

While the concept of sacrifice is present in religious texts, it is important to note that God does not require or condone the taking of human life. In fact, the commandment "thou shalt not kill" is one of the most fundamental teachings in many religious traditions. The value of human life is emphasized throughout the Bible and other religious traditions, and we are called to love and care for one another, not to harm or destroy each other.

As we reflect on the question of whether God requires the ultimate sacrifice of giving up one's life, we must consider the context and intention behind the concept of sacrifice. Sacrifice is not meant to be a violent or destructive act, but rather a way of expressing devotion and gratitude to God. It is a way of putting aside our own desires and priorities in order to align ourselves with God's will and purpose.

Reflective Question:

How can we reconcile the concept of sacrifice with the value of human life? What are some ways in which we can express our devotion to God without resorting to violence or harm to ourselves or others?

Original Text:

This is the lingering question in days of terrorist attacks and kamikaze raids. It is a day where innocent and unsuspecting people fall victim to the distorted concept that the ultimate honor to the "Almighty" is to die, as an expression of God's rage against an injustice within the social fiber of humanity.

Commentary:

This statement highlights the issue of terrorism and the use of violence in the name of religion. It questions the concept that the ultimate honor to God is to die as a martyr, and how this ideology has led to terrorist attacks and kamikaze raids, resulting in innocent people falling victim. It recognizes the distorted concept of using violence and sacrificing oneself as an expression of God's anger towards injustice within the social fabric of humanity.

Terrorism has become a major concern globally, with innocent people losing their lives due to the actions of extremist groups. The idea of giving up one's life as a form of sacrifice has been misused and distorted by those who claim to be serving God. This misinterpretation of religious teachings has led to the justification of acts of violence, including suicide bombings and other forms of terrorism, which have caused widespread destruction and loss of many lives.

It is important to recognize that God is a God of love and mercy, and that violence and the taking of innocent lives is never justified in His name. The concept of sacrifice in the scriptures refers to offering oneself as a living sacrifice, not as a literal sacrifice of one's life. It is a willingness to serve and give of one's self for the greater good, rather than taking the lives of others.

Reflective Question:

How can we as individuals and as a society address the issue of terrorism and violence perpetrated in the name of religion? What steps can we take to promote a message of love, peace, and tolerance, and to reject the distorted concept of using violence as an expression of God's will?

Original Text:

To live is to do that which is approved of Almighty God. It is too easy for God to remove his breath. We then, need not seek to remove it our self. So, it is with the following scriptures:

"O my lord! Grant me a righteous (son). So We gave him the good news of a boy (Isma'ili) ready to suffer and forebear. Then, when (the son) reached the age of serious work with him, he said: "O my son! I see in vision that I offer thee in sacrifice: Now see what is thy view! "The son said: "O my father! Do as thou art commanded: Thou wilt find me, if Allah so wills one practicing patience and constancy! So, when they had both submitted their wills to Allah and he had laid him prostrate on his forehead for sacrifice, we called out to him "O Abraham! Thou hast already fulfilled the vision!" Thus, indeed do We reward those who do right. For this was obviously a trial, and we ransomed him with a momentous sacrifice: and we left this blessing for him among generations to come in later times. "Peace and Salutation to Abraham!" This indeed do We reward those who do right: for he was one of our believing Servants. And We gave him the good

news of Isaac -a prophet- One of the Righteous. We blessed him and Isaac: but of their progeny are some that do right, and some that obviously do wrong, to their own souls. The Holy Qur'an, Surah 37:100-113.

While both father and son went up to Mount Moriah to present a sacrifice, the boy, Isaac, was correct to question his father, Abraham, about the absence of what would be the sacrifice.

Commentary:

The story of Abraham and his son being offered as a sacrifice in the Holy Qur'an and the Bible emphasizes the importance of submission to God's will and obedience to His commands. Both versions of the story highlight the willing-ness of a believer to surrender their own will and accept the trials and tests that come with it. Ismael and Isaac, the sons in each story, demonstrate their submission to God's will, even in the face of a difficult sacrifice.

Furthermore, the passages remind us that human life is a gift from God and should be valued and protected. Taking one's life or the lives of others is not within our authority, and we must respect and cherish the preciousness of life. Both religions teach that we must do no harm to ourselves or others and instead strive to do what is approved by Almighty God.

Reflective Question:

How can we submit to God's will in our daily lives and trust in His plan, even when it may be difficult or challenging? How can we appreciate and protect the gift of life that God has bestowed upon us?

Original Text:

Often time in depictions of this scriptural scene, Abraham is seen grasping the tool of sacrifice in a position to do harm to the boy. To read the aligning and subsequent scriptures is to understand the action occurring prior to the Angel's call to Abraham. Genesis 22:10 states: And Abraham stretched forth his hand and took the knife to slay his son. As one is bringing his/her hand toward an object, is the action taking place? Abraham's hand only grasped the knife and his hand stayed in that position; upon his hearing the Angel speak. Abraham, then, was prohibited from even a threatening gesture of a raised knife over his son but rather, the distractions prevailed, and the true object of sacrifice revealed: a "prepared" ram caught in the thicket.

Commentary:

The story of Abraham and Isaac's sacrifice is one of the most well-known and often-discussed stories in both the Bible and the Quran. This particular passage draws attention to the common misinterpretation of Abraham's actions during the sacrifice, where he is often depicted as about to harm his son. In reality, the scriptures make it clear that Abraham's actions were only up to the point of "preparing" or "displaying" Isaac as a sacrifice, rather than actually causing harm to Isaac.

This passage reminds us of the importance of reading and interpreting scripture accurately, without imposing our own biases or preconceptions onto the text. It highlights the fact that even the most well-known stories can be misinterpreted or misunderstood, and that we must be diligent in our efforts to understand the true meaning of the texts.

Reflective Question:

How can we ensure that we are reading and interpreting scripture accurately, and not imposing our own biases onto the text? What steps can we take to approach scripture with an open and unbiased mind?

Original Text:

Even so and while not spared the agony of the journey to Mount Moriah, the development and arrangement of the altar, and the placement of Isaac thereupon, Abraham's obedience was tested only to the point of "preparing" or "displaying" Isaac as a sacrifice, rather than making or causing him to be the sacrifice. In other words, God's provision was implied in how he directed Abraham: to "offer" rather than "make" Isaac a sacrifice.

Commentary:

The story of Abraham and Isaac is one of the most famous and profound stories in the Bible, and it is often used as a metaphor for the ultimate test of faith. It is a story of sacrifice, obedience, and trust, and it is a powerful reminder of the importance of submitting to God's will.

In this passage, the author highlights an important distinction in the story: Abraham was directed to "offer" Isaac as a sacrifice, not to "make" him a sacrifice. This implies that God's provision was already in place and that the ultimate goal was not for Isaac to be killed, but for Abraham's obedience to be tested.

This distinction is important because it shows that God does not require us to harm ourselves or others in order to prove our faith or loyalty. Rather, He tests us in ways that allow us to grow and develop as individuals and as believers.

Abraham's obedience to God's command to offer Isaac as a sacrifice was a powerful testament to his faith, and it served as a model for future generations of believers. The story of

Abraham and Isaac continues to inspire and challenge us to-day, reminding us that the ultimate test of faith is not in what we are willing to give up, but in our willingness to submit to God's will.

Reflective Question:

How do you respond when faced with a difficult test of faith or obedience? Do you trust in God's provision and submit to His will, or do you struggle to hold on to your own desires and plans?

Original Text:

Therefore, and as God manifested the essence of his love to-ward both Abraham and Isaac in this scriptural depiction, it is significant to note specifically what was spoken prior to (offer a sacrifice) and while upon Mount Moriah, "do the child no harm" (this to ones' self-and/or toward others) that ultimately gives weight to the event.

Commentary:

This statement emphasizes the message that God values and cherishes human life, and that we should follow this example by not causing harm to ourselves or others. This concept is reiterated throughout many religious texts, including the Bible and the Qur'an.

In the story of Abraham and Isaac, we see the importance of valuing human life and the great lengths that God went to show His love and protection for His people. God provided a ram for Abraham to sacrifice instead of his son, demonstrating that He does not require us to harm ourselves or others to show our devotion to Him.

As believers, we are called to follow this example and to treat all human life with respect and dignity. We should strive to avoid causing harm or pain to ourselves or others, recognizing that each life is precious and valuable in the eyes of God.

Reflective Question:

How can we apply the message of valuing and protecting human life in our daily lives? In what ways can we demonstrate love and compassion for others while avoiding causing harm?

Conclusion: Do No Harm to Self or Others

The concept of sacrifice is a complex and multifaceted topic that has been discussed and debated for centuries. The story of Abraham and Isaac serves as a powerful reminder of the importance of obedience to God's commands and the need to value and protect human life. We must be diligent in our efforts to read and interpret scripture accurately, without imposing our own biases or preconceptions onto the text. As believers, we are called to submit to God's will and to trust in His provision, even when it may be difficult or challenging. We must strive to do no harm to ourselves or others and to demonstrate love and compassion for all. May we all take the lessons learned from this chapter and apply them in our daily lives, seeking to honor God and live in harmony with one another.

Chapter 26

It Is Not for You

Psalm 62:10

The cited scripture speaks to those who govern or have rule over others. Herein are three prohibitions that delete themselves as weapons for governance.

Oppression is to subject individuals to a harsh or cruel form of domination; to be a source of worry, stress, or trouble to others. Even more is to be excessively proud when one succeeds in schemes of robbery wherein the people are given to poverty for the contentment of zealous greed. Finally, and where one's riches increase as a result of popularity, it is not a good thing to set your heart, your desire, your being upon riches. This, too, shall pass and often as fast as it was obtained.

It seems the balance is the command to trust the Lord with all your heart, and lean not unto your own understanding, but in all your ways acknowledge him and he shall direct your path; a path of governance that is divinely directed, and pleasing before God and man.

Introduction: It Is Not for You

In Psalm 62:10, we are reminded of the responsibilities that come with governance and leadership. This passage highlights three prohibitions that leaders should avoid: oppression, schemes of robbery, and setting one's heart upon riches. These actions are destructive not only to those who are being governed but also to the leaders themselves. Instead, leaders are called to trust in the Lord and to seek divine direction in their governance. This chapter delves into the significance of these prohibitions and explores how leaders can implement a divine approach to governance that is pleasing to God and beneficial to all. By doing so, they can uphold the value of human life and dignity, and ensure that their leadership is in service to the greater good.

Psalm 62:10

"Trust not in oppression, and become not vain in robbery: if riches increase, set not your heart upon them.

Original Text:
The cited scripture speaks to those who govern or have rule over others. Herein are three prohibitions that delete themselves as weapons for governance.

Commentary:
Psalm 62:10 is a powerful scripture that speaks directly to those who have positions of power and authority over others. The verse provides three clear prohibitions that should not be used as weapons for governance: oppression, extortion, and pride. These three actions are all too common in human history, and they have been used as tools for control and domination over others throughout the centuries.

The first prohibition is oppression, which involves subjecting individuals to harsh or cruel domination. Oppression can take many forms, including physical, emotional, and psychological abuse. It is a tool of control that is often used by those in power to maintain their authority and keep others "in line". However, the Bible teaches that this kind of behavior is not pleasing to God and should not be used as a weapon for governance.

The second prohibition is extortion, which involves obtaining wealth or other benefits through illegal or unethical means. This kind of behavior is often seen in corrupt systems of governance, where those in power use their positions to enrich themselves at the expense of others. However, the Bible teaches that this kind of behavior is not pleasing to God and is ultimately self-destructive.

The third prohibition is pride, which involves excessive self-confidence and arrogance. This kind of behavior is often seen in leaders who are more interested in their own glory and success than in serving their people. However, the Bible teaches that this kind of behavior is not pleasing to God and can lead to downfall.

Reflective Question:

How can we ensure that those in positions of power and authority use their positions for good and not for personal gain? How can we hold our leaders accountable for their actions and ensure that they govern with integrity and righteousness?

Original Text:

This passage speaks to the dangers of oppression and the negative effects it can have on both the oppressor and the oppressed. It highlights the idea that excessive pride and greed can lead to schemes of robbery and exploitation, ultimately resulting in poverty and suffering for those who are marginalized and oppressed.

Commentary:

Oppression is a form of domination that seeks to maintain power and control over others through force or manipulation. It can manifest in many different ways, from systemic racism and discrimination to individual acts of bullying or abuse. Regardless of the form it takes, oppression is a destructive force that causes harm to both the oppressed and the oppressor.

The passage also warns against the dangers of excessive pride and greed, which can lead to a willingness to exploit and harm others in pursuit of personal gain. This can take the form of schemes of robbery and theft, where the rich become richer at the expense of the poor. It can also lead to a focus on material wealth and possessions, which ultimately prove fleeting and temporary.

In contrast to these negative qualities, the passage encourages a focus on humility, compassion, and generosity. By recognizing the value and dignity of all individuals, regardless of their social or economic status, we can work towards building a more just and equitable society. By avoiding the temptation

to exploit or harm others for personal gain, we can cultivate a sense of mutual respect and cooperation that benefits
everyone.

Reflective Question:

How can we recognize and resist oppression in our daily
lives, and what can we do to promote a more just and equitable society? How can we cultivate humility, compassion,
and generosity in our interactions with others, and avoid the
temptations of excessive pride and greed?

Original Text:

*It seems the balance is the command to trust the Lord with
all your heart, and lean not unto your own understanding, but in
all your ways acknowledge Him and He shall direct your path; a
path of governance that is divinely directed, and pleasing before
God and man.*

Commentary:

The balance of power for those who govern or have rule
over others lies in their ability to trust in the Lord and seek
His guidance in their decisions. The verse from Proverbs 3:5-6,
"Trust in the Lord with all your heart and lean not on your
own understanding; in all your ways submit to him, and he
will make your paths straight," emphasizes the importance of
surrendering one's own will and desires to God and relying on
His wisdom and guidance. This is particularly crucial for those
in positions of power, as their decisions can have a significant
impact on the lives of those they govern.

By acknowledging God in all their ways, those in power
can ensure their decisions are divinely directed and pleasing
to both God and man. Therefore, it is essential for those who
govern to recognize their authority and success are not solely
dependent on their own capabilities, but on their submission

to God's will. This humble attitude also serves as a safeguard against pride that can weasel in with success, and ultimately assure the presence of oppressive, greedy, and unconcern for those to whom God has given power to govern over His people.

Reflective Question:

How can I apply the principle of trusting in God and acknowledging Him in all my ways to my own life, even if I am not in a position of power or governance?

Conclusion: It Is Not for You

Psalm 62:10 reminds us of the weighty responsibilities that come with leadership and governance, and the dangers of using oppression, extortion, and pride as tools for control. Instead, leaders are called to trust in the Lord and seek divine guidance in their decisions, cultivating humility, compassion, and generosity in their interactions with others. By doing so, they can promote a more just and equitable society that upholds the value and dignity of all individuals. As we reflect on this passage, let us consider how we can hold our leaders accountable for their actions and promote a path of governance that is divinely directed and pleasing before God and man.

Chapter 27

The Experience of Communing with God

Matthew 19:29

Father Abraham is a fitting example of the premium placed on forsaking all for the sake of communing with Almighty God. Abram, who ultimately became Abraham and the father of nations, did not simply leave what was his, but he captured the essence of a monotheistic relationship that looked beyond the visible into the invisible and made a profound discovery.

The discovery was there really is nothing except He who was, is, and will always be. It is not too difficult to imagine Abraham looking into a starry filled night and asking, "Who are you" rather than "Where are you". The response no doubt proved overwhelming as he vividly heard a soft voice say, "I am, that I am." To this experience were others of like magnitude such that Abraham longed the consumption of more and more time; thereby, leaving the mundane to ministry, and mastering the message of faith that addresses needs and fulfills purpose.

Thus, it was these moments, times and conversations that led him to desire more time, more opportunity, more space to commune with the permanents', presence, and personality of a friend he came to know through the closeness of quiet solitude. Within this silence was the absence of Abraham's thought of houses, brethren, sisters, father, mother, wife's, children or lands.

It is daily experiences that distract or inhibit one's focus and restrains the desire to commune with God. However, and because it is He who has ordained family and given man dominion over the works of His hand that God does not condemn family relations, nor ownership of tangible assets. Instead, the call is for a daily oneness with He who was, is and will always be, least we take hold of that which secures less value in comparison with the wealth that brings a hundredfold, and assures everlasting life.

Introduction: The Experience of Communing with God

The "Experience of Communing with God" is a topic that has fascinated seekers of truth and spiritual enlightenment for centuries. The Bible provides numerous examples of individuals who have had profound experiences with God, but perhaps none more so than Father Abraham. Abraham's journey of faith is marked by his willingness to forsake all for the sake of communing with God; a decision that ultimately led to him becoming the father of nations.

Through his experiences with God, Abraham discovered the essence of a monotheistic relationship that looked beyond the visible into the invisible. He came to the realization that there really is nothing except for "He who was, is, and will always be". These experiences led him to desire more time, more opportunity, more space to commune with God, and to leave behind the mundane to minister and fulfill his purpose.

This chapter explores the significance of Abraham's experiences and what they can teach us about communing with God. It will also address the distractions and obstacles that can inhibit our focus and desire to commune with God in our daily lives. Ultimately, it will emphasize the importance of seeking oneness with God, lest we take hold of that which secures less value in comparison with the wealth that brings a hundredfold and assures everlasting life. Matthew 19:29 reminds us of the rewards that await those who are willing to forsake all for the sake of communing with God.

Matthew 19:29

And every one that hath forsaken houses, or brethren, or sisters, or father, or mother, or wife, or children, or lands, for my name's sake, shall receive a hundredfold, and shall inherit everlasting life.

Original Text:

Father Abraham is a fitting example of the premium placed on forsaking all for the sake of communing with Almighty God. Abram, who ultimately became Abraham and the father of nations, did not simply leave what was his, but he captured the essence of a monotheistic relationship that looked beyond the visible into the invisible and made a profound discovery.

Commentary:

Abraham, or Abram as he was originally named, is a significant figure in the Bible and is regarded as the father of the Jewish people. He is also highly regarded in Christianity and Islam. One of the key themes in Abraham's story is his willingness to forsake everything for the sake of communing with God. This is evident in his decision to leave his homeland and his family to follow God's call to a new land.

Abraham's decision to leave everything behind was not simply a matter of physical relocation. Rather, it was a spiritual journey that involved a deepening relationship with God. Through his journey, Abraham captured the essence of a monotheistic relationship that looked beyond the visible into the invisible and made a profound discovery. He discovered that God was not just a deity to be worshipped, but a personal God who desired a relationship with his people.

This relationship was not limited to the physical realm but extended into the spiritual realm. Abraham communed with God through prayer, meditation, and obedience to God's commands. His faith in God was tested time and time again, and through each trial, he grew closer to God.

Abraham's story is a powerful reminder of the importance of forsaking all for the sake of communing with God. It highlights the value of a deep, personal relationship with God that transcends physical possessions and circumstances. It also serves as an example of the transformative power of faith, and the ways in which God can work in the lives of those who seek Him with all their heart.

Reflective Question:
How can we follow Abraham's example of forsaking all for the sake of communing with God? What steps can we take to deepen our relationship with God and experience His transformative power in our lives?

Original Text:
The discovery was there really is nothing except He who was, is, and will always be. It is not too difficult to imagine Abraham looking into a starry-filled night and asking, "Who are you" rather than "Where are you". The response no doubt proved overwhelming as he vividly heard a soft voice say, "I am, that I am." To this experience were others of like magnitude such that Abraham longed the consumption of more and more time; thereby, leaving the mundane to ministry and mastering the message of faith to address needs and fulfill purpose.

Commentary:
The experience of Abraham communing with God was not just a one-time event but a continuous journey of discovering the divine. Abraham's encounter with God was not just an intellectual exercise but a spiritual awakening that transformed his entire being. The discovery that there really is nothing except He who was, is, and will always be, is a profound realization that changes one's perspective on life and the world.

It is not difficult to imagine Abraham gazing into the starry night sky and contemplating the vastness and beauty of the universe. In this moment of wonder and awe, Abraham's curiosity led him to ask not just "Where are you?" but more profoundly, "Who are you?" The answer he received was overwhelming and transformative, as he heard a soft voice say,

"I am, that I am." This revelation led Abraham to seek more experiences of God's presence and to dedicate more time to communing with Him.

Abraham's desire for more communion with God led him to leave behind the mundane aspects of life, focus on ministry and fulfill his purpose. He became a master of the message of faith and addressed the needs of those around him. This deepened his relationship with God and allowed him to fulfill his divine purpose.

Reflective Question:

How can we cultivate a deeper relationship with God and seek more experiences of His presence in our daily lives? How can we leave behind the mundane and focus on fulfilling our divine purpose?

Original Text:

Thus, it was these moments, times and conversations that led him to desire more time, more opportunity, more space to commune with the preeminent, presence, and person of a friend he came to know through the closeness of quiet solitude. Within this silence was the absence of thought of houses, or brethren, or sisters, or father, or mother, or wives, or children, or lands.

Commentary:

The commentary on this passage is a reminder of the importance of carving out time and space to connect with God in quiet solitude. Abraham's desire to commune with God was so strong that he longed for more time and opportunity to be in God's presence. In this state of quiet solitude, Abraham was able to focus solely on God, without distractions or thoughts of worldly possessions and relationships.

This passage challenges us to consider our own priorities and the ways in which we spend our time. It is easy to become consumed with worldly pursuits and the distractions of daily life, leaving little time and space for quiet communion with God. However, Abraham's example reminds us that connecting with God in solitude is essential for spiritual growth and fulfilling our purpose.

Furthermore, the absence of thought of houses, brethren, sisters, father, mother, wife, children, or lands highlights the need for detachment from material possessions and relationships. While these things are important, they should not consume our thoughts and distract us from our relationship with God. Instead, our focus should be on cultivating a deeper connection with God and living out our purpose in service to Him.

Reflective Question:

How can we create more time and space for quiet communion with God in our daily lives? How can we detach ourselves from worldly distractions and prioritize our relationship with God above all else?

Original Text:

It is daily experiences that distract or inhibit one's focus and restrains the desire to commune with God. However, and because it is He who has ordained family and given man dominion over the works of His hand, that God does not condemn family relations nor ownership of tangible assets. Instead, the call is for a daily oneness with He who was, is and will always be, least we take hold of that which secures less value in comparison with the wealth that brings a hundredfold, and assures everlasting life.

Commentary:

The desire to commune with God is often hindered by the distractions and busyness of daily life. While family and material possessions are important, they can easily become the focus of one's attention, drawing away from the pursuit of a deeper relationship with God. However, it is important to recognize that God has ordained family relationships and given humans dominion over the works of His hand. Therefore, the call is not to abandon these relationships or possessions but to seek a daily oneness with God, recognizing that He is the ultimate source of value and fulfillment.

In Matthew 6:33, Jesus instructs his disciples to "seek first the kingdom of God and his righteousness, and all these things will be added to you." This passage emphasizes the importance of prioritizing our relationship with God above all else. By seeking God first, we can find true fulfillment and purpose in life, and all other things will fall into place.

Reflective Question:

How can we maintain a daily oneness with God amidst the distractions and busyness of daily life? How can we ensure that our pursuit of family and material possessions does not hinder our pursuit of a deeper relationship with God? How can we seek first the kingdom of God in all aspects of our lives?

Conclusion: The Experience of Communing with God

The experience of communing with God is a journey of discovery and transformation that requires forsaking all for the sake of deepening one's relationship with Him. Abraham's example teaches us the importance of seeking God in quiet solitude, detaching ourselves from worldly distractions, and prioritizing our relationship with Him above all else. While family and material possessions are important, they should not consume our thoughts or distract us from our pursuit of God. Instead, we should seek a daily oneness with God, recognizing that He is the ultimate source of value and fulfillment in our lives. Reflecting on Abraham's example, how can we prioritize our relationship with God in our daily lives and cultivate a deeper connection with Him?

Chapter 28

The Drama Before
the Crucifixion

John 5:25

At first glance and without a thorough reading of this scripture, verse 25 is often mistaken to imply that the dead shall hear the voice of the son of Mary, but it is only those that hear shall live. The verse poses an excellent example for the need of reading, meditating and studying scripture, if it is to be "rightly divided."

It is this chapter that provides the drama preceding the crucifixion appearance of Jesus. It is in this chapter the depth of disdain harbored by the Jewish leadership against Jesus is detected. It is as though the leaderships' assigned people monitored and reported Jesus' every action and movement. So much so that miracles were suspect as charges and traditions were misused despite benefit.

These surveillances were a pretext to levy a serious charge that would warrant the death penalty. Thus, and as documented in verses 16 and 18, the Jewish leadership resolved the charge and justification to proceed with a plan to seize Jesus of Nazareth.

Notwithstanding the scheme, Jesus myopically expresses his purpose, practice and power over life and punishment, his treatise culminating in the essence of this authority over not simply the lame man at the Bethesda Pool but his authority over all humanity, even those in the grave.

When Jesus mentions the hour is coming, his context engulfs a future realm while the words "and now is" speak to this present authority to quicken. These three words give defense for the miracle at the Bethesda Pool as attested by the multitude but ignored by the Jewish leadership.

Even so, the clarity of verse 28 substantiates Jesus' authority over all humanity and sustains that all who are in the graves shall hear the voice of the Son of God and shall come forth or be resurrected; some unto life, some unto damnation.

Without mistake, the understanding of this scripture is that everybody shall hear His voice and in hearing shall be resurrected and quicken. For they that hear shall live to have consciousness to discern their fate; a fate of reward or a fate of punishment.

Introduction: The Drama Before the Crucifixion

The Drama Before the Crucifixion is a story in the Bible that provides a glimpse into the events leading up to the crucifixion of Jesus. At the heart of this drama is the deep-seated disdain that the Jewish leadership harbored against Jesus, which led them to monitor his every movement and action. Despite the benefit of his miracles, they misused tradition and levied a serious charge that warranted the death penalty.

In this chapter, Jesus myopically expresses his purpose, practice, and power over life and punishment. He speaks to his authority over not just the lame man at the Bethesda Pool but over all humanity, even those in the grave. His words give a defense for the miracle at the Bethesda Pool, attested to by the multitude but ignored by the Jewish leadership.

Verse 28 clarifies Jesus' authority over all humanity, affirming that all who are in the graves shall hear the voice of the Son of God and shall come forth or be resurrected, some unto life and some unto damnation. This scripture reminds us that everybody shall hear His voice and, in hearing, shall be resurrected and quickened. It is a powerful reminder of the importance of studying and meditating on scripture to gain a deeper understanding of its meaning.

John 5:25:

Verily, verily, I say unto you, the hour is coming, and now is, when the dead shall hear the voice of the Son of God: and they that hear shall live.

Original Text:

At first glance and without a thorough reading of this scripture, verse 25 is often mistaken to imply that the dead shall hear the voice of the son of Mary, but it is only those that hear shall live. The verse poses an excellent example for the need of reading, meditating and studying and scripture, if it is to be "rightly divided."

Commentary:

The opening **Commentary** of this chapter highlights the importance of reading, meditating, and studying scripture to fully understand its meaning. John 5:25 is a perfect example of how a surface-level reading of a scripture can lead to a misunderstanding of its true meaning.

At first glance, the verse may seem to suggest that the dead shall hear the voice of the son of Mary. However, upon closer examination, it becomes clear that the verse is referring only to those who hear the voice of the son of Mary as being able to live. This highlights the importance of careful reading and interpretation of scripture, as well as the need for deeper reflection and study to fully understand its meaning.

Reflective Question:

How can we ensure that we are reading, meditating, and studying scripture in a way that allows us to understand its true meaning? What practices can we implement to deepen our understanding of the Bible?

Original Text:

It is this chapter that provides the drama preceding the crucifixion appearance of Jesus. It is in this chapter the depth of disdain harbored by the Jewish leadership against Jesus is detected. It is as though the leaderships' assigned people monitored and reported Jesus' every action and movement. So much so that miracles were suspect as charges and tradition misused despite benefit.

Commentary:

The fifth chapter of the Gospel of John provides a dramatic and pivotal moment leading up to Jesus' crucifixion. It is in this chapter that we see the depth of disdain harbored by the Jewish leaders against Jesus. The religious leaders were so suspicious of Jesus that they assigned people to monitor and report his every action and movement. Despite the miracles he performed and the benefit they provided; the Jewish leadership misused their traditions to charge Jesus with blasphemy.

The tension between Jesus and the religious leaders is evident in their interactions throughout the chapter. Jesus performs a miraculous healing at the Bethesda pool, but instead of rejoicing at the healing, the Jewish leaders question the legitimacy of Jesus' actions. This leads to a confrontation between Jesus and the religious leaders, with Jesus defending his authority and identity as the Son of God.

The chapter also serves as a reminder of the dangers of religious legalism and the importance of recognizing the true spirit and intention behind religious traditions. The religious leaders in this chapter were so focused on upholding their traditions and laws that they failed to recognize and/or refused to believe in the true power and authority of Jesus as the Son of God.

Reflective Question:

How can we guard against falling into the trap of religious legalism and instead focus on the true spirit and intention behind our religious traditions? In what ways can we learn from the mistakes of the Jewish leaders in this chapter and cultivate a deeper understanding and appreciation of the true power and authority of Jesus in our lives?

Original Text:

These surveillances were a pretext to levy a serious charge that would warrant the death penalty. Thus, and as documented in verses 16 and 18, the Jewish leadership resolved the charge and justification to proceed with a plan to seize Jesus of Nazareth.

Commentary:

In John 5, we see the Jewish leadership's growing hostility towards Jesus, which ultimately leads to his crucifixion. The leadership had assigned people to monitor Jesus' every action and movement, suspecting that his miracles were somehow fraudulent or deceitful. Despite the obvious benefits of Jesus' ministry, the Jewish leaders continued to view him with suspicion and disdain.

This deep-seated hostility towards Jesus ultimately led to a plan to seize him, which is documented in verses 16 and 18. The charges brought against Jesus were serious enough to warrant the death penalty, indicating just how determined the Jewish leadership was to rid themselves of this perceived threat.

The situation described in John 5 serves as a cautionary tale about the dangers of prejudice and preconceived notions. The Jewish leadership was so convinced of their own rightness and so fearful of any threat to their power that they were willing to go to great lengths to silence Jesus.

This story also raises questions about the nature of power and authority. Who has the right to wield power, and how should that power be used? Is it ever acceptable to use violence or force to silence someone with whom we disagree? These are complex ethical questions that continue to be debated today.

Reflective Question:

How can we guard against the dangers of prejudice and pre-conceived notions in our own lives? How can we ensure that our actions are guided by a desire for truth and justice, rather than a desire to maintain power or control?

Original Text:
Notwithstanding the scheme, Jesus myopically expresses his purpose, practice and power over life and punishment, his treatise culminating in the essence of this authority over not simply the lame man ant the Bethesda Pool but his authority over all humanity, even those in the grave.

Commentary:
In this passage, we see Jesus asserting His power and authority over all aspects of life and death. Despite the schemes of the Jewish leadership to condemn Him, Jesus focuses on expressing His purpose and demonstrating His power. He emphasizes His ability to give life, heal the sick, and pass judgment on those who have done wrong.

The healing of the lame man at the Bethesda Pool serves as a powerful symbol of Jesus' power and authority. By healing the man who had been paralyzed for 38 years, Jesus shows that He has the power to give life and restore health. This miracle also reveals His compassion and concern for those who are suffering and marginalized.

Moreover, Jesus' power and authority extend beyond physical healing. He also has the power to judge and pass sentences on those who have done wrong. His message culminates in the essence of His authority over all humanity, even those in the grave. This emphasizes that His power is not limited to the physical realm but extends into the spiritual realm as well.

Reflective Question:

How can we come to a deeper understanding of Jesus' power and authority over all aspects of life and death? How can we incorporate this knowledge into our daily lives to live in greater faith and obedience?

Original Text:

When Jesus mentions the hour is coming, his context engulfs a future realm while the words "and now is" speak to this present authority to quicken. These three words give defense for the miracle at the Bethesda Pool as attested by the multitude but ignored by the Jewish leadership.

Commentary:

In John 5, Jesus mentions that the hour is coming when the dead shall hear the voice of the Son of God, and those who hear shall live. This statement reveals Jesus' authority over life and death, and the promise of resurrection for all who believe in Him. However, it is important to note that Jesus also speaks in the present tense, saying "and now is" to emphasize His present authority to quicken.

The words "and now is" refer to the fact that Jesus had the power to heal the lame man at the Bethesda Pool, as attested by the multitude who witnessed the miracle. However, the Jewish leaders chose to ignore this evidence and instead focused on their own agenda to condemn Jesus. This highlights the contrast between those who recognize Jesus' authority and those who reject it.

Jesus' statement about the hour coming also reveals His understanding of a future realm beyond our present reality. He speaks of a time when all who are in the graves shall hear His voice and come forth, some to life and some to damnation. This speaks to the ultimate authority of Jesus over all of humanity, both in the present and in the future.

Reflective Question:

How can we recognize and respond to the present authority of Jesus in our daily lives? How can we ensure that we are not ignoring or dismissing the evidence of His power and authority? And how can we prepare ourselves for the future realm that Jesus speaks of?

Commentary:

Even so, the clarity of verse 28 substantiates Jesus' authority over all humanity and sustains that all who are in the graves shall hear the voice of the Son of God and shall come forth or be resurrected; some unto life, some unto damnation.

Commentary:

In John 5:28, Jesus asserts his ultimate authority over all of humanity, stating that all who are in the graves shall hear his voice and come forth, some unto life and some unto damnation. This verse highlights Jesus' role as the ultimate judge of humanity, who will determine each person's eternal fate.

The concept of resurrection is a central theme in Christianity, as it represents the belief in life after death and the promise of eternal life. Jesus' authority over resurrection demonstrates his divine power and highlights the importance of faith in his teachings.

The phrase "some unto life, some unto damnation" underscores the idea of judgment and the consequences of one's actions in life. It serves as a warning that our choices and actions in life will determine our ultimate destiny. This verse emphasizes the importance of living a righteous life and following Jesus' teachings in order to attain salvation and avoid eternal damnation.

Reflective Question:

How does the concept of resurrection and judgment in John 5:28 impact your personal faith and actions in life? What steps can you take to ensure that your choices align with Jesus' teachings and lead to eternal life?

Original Text:

Without mistake, the understanding of this scripture is that everybody shall hear His voice and in hearing shall be resurrected and quicken. For they that hear shall live to have consciousness to discern their fate a fate of reward or a fate of punishment.

Commentary:

In this passage, the idea of resurrection and judgment is central to Jesus' teachings. The verse affirms that everyone, both the righteous and the wicked, will be resurrected and will face judgment according to their deeds. This teaching was radical in Jesus' time as the Jewish belief was that only the righteous would be resurrected.

Jesus' message is clear those who hear his voice and believe in him will have eternal life, but those who reject him will face judgment and eternal punishment. This is a warning that one should not take their relationship with God lightly, and that one must heed Jesus' words and teachings to secure their eternal destiny.

Reflective Question:

How does this passage challenge our beliefs about resurrection and judgment? How can we use this message to deepen our relationship with God and ensure our eternal destiny?

Conclusion: The Drama Before the Crucifixion

The Drama before the Crucifixion in the fifth chapter of the Gospel of John provides a powerful reminder of the importance of reading, meditating, and studying scripture in order to gain a deeper understanding of its meaning. It also highlights the dangers of prejudice, preconceived notions, and religious legalism, and emphasizes the importance of recognizing the true spirit and intention behind religious traditions. The chapter reveals Jesus' authority over all aspects of life and death, and the promise of resurrection for all who believe in Him. It also warns of the consequences of rejecting Jesus' teachings and emphasizes the importance of living a righteous life to attain salvation and avoid eternal damnation. Reflecting on these themes can deepen our faith and help us live a life guided by truth and justice.

Chapter 29

Keep My Judgments and Do Them

Ezekiel 20:9

What is it that God requires of us daily? It is to know His statutes and keep his judgments.

From the Zohar is a Kabbalistic story about shattering of the vessels and the gathering of sparks (Patterson, David. Greatest Jewish Stories, Jonathan David Publishers, Inc. Middle Village, New York, 2001). A depiction of the story reads as follows:

Long before the luminaries of the heavens were created, long before the holy word brought heaven and earth into being, a flame arose from a single point so small as to be invisible. From the depth of that flame sparks of light burst forth and were placed in vessels. These vessels carried the light, which was the light of holiness, into all the spheres of heaven and earth, like ships bearing a cargo more precious than diamonds. But the light was too much for the vessels. They broke into bits, and the light was scattered throughout the world.

To know His statutes is to read, study, meditate and apply the scriptures without deviation, in the governance of one's own life and those as He has stationed, and according to the precepts (biblical and others) left throughout the ages. To this is also commanded the keeping of His judgments, which is to remain mindful of the benefits of life: paradise, and the consequences of death: damnation in the present and end times. The command, finally, is to do both as individual and collective daily actions, forsaking them not, for approval of Him who has committed this saying for the benefit of humanity.

When kept are His statutes and judgments, this action is equivalent to knowing one's purpose: to search for the sparks of light, wherever they may be, and raise them to holiness. Once all the sparks of the divine light have been collected, the vessels that once contained them will be restored.

Often is the evidence of God to provide a clear mapping of His expectation of man. This mapping painstakingly outlines the path to success; its' boundaries aligned with dignity and the knowledge that every step is a true orchestration of redemption; a redemption that levels the playing field for achieving ones intended purpose here on earth. It is the expectation of restoration to all waiting to rejoice at the return of the Messiah.

Introduction: Keep My Judgement and Do Them

In Ezekiel 20:9, God instructs us to know His statutes, keep His judgments, and to do both. These commands are not suggestions, but requirements for those who seek to follow and please Him. The Zohar, a Kabbalistic text, tells a story of the shattering of vessels and the gathering of sparks of light. This story emphasizes the importance of seeking out and gathering these sparks of divine light, which were scattered throughout the world when the vessels that contained them broke.

To know God's statutes (sparks) us to read, study, meditate, and apply the scriptures without deviation; using them to govern our lives and the lives of those around us. Keeping His judgments means remaining mindful of the consequences of our actions and striving to live a righteous and holy life. These actions, done both individually and collectively, help us to fulfill our purpose in searching for and raising up the sparks of divine light and thereby, restore the vessels that once contained them.

God's commands are not meant to restrict us, but to guide us towards a life of purpose and fulfillment. By following His statutes and keeping His judgments, we align ourselves with His will and bring ourselves closer to Him. The expectation of restoration and the return of the Messiah is the ultimate goal of these commands, as we wait eagerly for the day when all will be made right.

Ezekiel 20:9

But I wrought for my name's sake, that it should not be polluted before the heathen, among whom they were, in whose sight I made myself known unto them, in bringing them forth out of the land of Egypt.

Original Text:

What is it that God requires of us daily? It is to both know His statutes, keep His commandments and acknowledge His judgments.

Commentary:

In Ezekiel 20:9, God sets out the requirement for his people to know His statutes, keep His judgments, and do both on a daily basis. To know God's statutes is to have a deepened understanding of His commandments, precepts, and teachings. This involves reading and studying the scriptures, meditating on their meaning, and applying them to one's daily life. It is not enough to simply know God's statutes, as one must also keep His judgments. Keeping God's judgments involve being mindful of the consequences of one's actions and striving to live a life that is aligned with God's will.

The call of this scripture is a reminder that knowledge without action is meaningless. It is not enough to know God's statutes and judgments; one must also act on this knowledge and live a life that is pleasing to God. This awareness requires a commitment to obedience, self-discipline, and a willingness to make sacrifices for the sake of God's will.

Reflective Question:

How can we ensure not simply "hearing" the word of God, but actively "doing" His will? What practical steps can we take to cultivate a deeper understanding of God's statutes and judgments, and to live a life aligned with His will?

Original Text:

From the Zohar is a Kabbalistic story about shattering of the vessels and the gathering of sparks (Patterson, David. Greatest Jewish Stories, Jonathan David Publishers, Inc. Middle Village, New York, 2001). A depiction of the story reads as follows:

Long before the luminaries of the heavens were created, long before the holy word brought heaven and earth into being, a flame arose from a single point so small as to be invisible. From the depth of that flame sparks of light burst forth and were placed in vessels. These vessels carried the light, which was the light of holiness, into all the spheres of heaven and earth, like ships bearing a cargo more precious than diamonds. But the light was too much for the vessels. They broke into bits, and the light was scattered throughout the world.

Commentary:

The Zohar is a Kabbalistic text that contains mystical interpretations of the Torah and other Jewish texts. It is believed to have been written in the 13th century by the Spanish Jewish mystic Moses de Leon. The Zohar teaches that the Torah contains hidden meanings that can be unlocked through the study of Kabbalah.

One of the stories in the Zohar is about the shattering of vessels and the gathering of sparks. According to the story, long before the creation of the luminaries of the heavens and the holy word that brought heaven and earth into being, a flame arose from a single point so small that it was invisible. From the depth of that flame, sparks of light burst forth and were placed in vessels. These vessels carried the light of holiness into all the spheres of heaven and earth, like ships bearing a cargo more precious than diamonds. But the light was too much for the vessels, and they broke into bits, scattering the light throughout the world.

This story has been interpreted in many different ways, but one common interpretation is that it represents the human soul, which is a spark of the divine light that has been scattered throughout the world. The vessels that carried the light represent the physical world, which is a container for the divine spark. The shattering of the vessels represents the fall of humanity and the scattering of the divine spark through-out the world. The gathering of sparks represents the work of the soul to find and reunite with the divine spark, and the restoration of the vessels represents the ultimate redemption of humanity.

In the context of the requirement to know God's statutes and keep His judgments, the story of the shattering of vessels and the gathering of sparks can be seen as a call to seek out and reunite with the divine spark that is within us. By study-ing and applying God's statutes and judgments, we can begin to gather the scattered sparks of the divine light and restore the vessels that contain them. This work is an ongoing process that requires daily effort and dedication.

Reflective Question:

How can we apply the story of the shattering of vessels and the gathering of sparks in our daily lives to deepen our under-standing of God's statutes and judgments? How can we work to gather the scattered sparks of the divine light within us and restore the vessels that contain them?

Original Text:

To know His statutes is to read, study, meditate and apply the scriptures without deviation, in the governance of one's own life and those as He has stationed, and according to the precepts (biblical and others) left throughout the ages. To this is also commanded the keeping of His judgments, which is to remain mindful of the benefits of life: paradise, and the consequences of death: damnation in the present and end times. The command, finally, is to do both as individual and collective daily actions, forsaking them not, for approval from Him who has committed this saying for benefit of humanity.

Commentary:

The passage emphasizes the importance of knowing and keeping God's statutes and judgments. To know His statutes is not simply to read the Bible, but to study it, meditate on it, and apply it in one's daily life. This requires a deep understanding of the precepts left throughout the ages, not just biblical ones, but also those from other sources that align with God's teachings. It is a command that requires diligence, discipline, and a determination to forsake one's own desires in favor of obedience to God's will.

Keeping God's judgments means being mindful of the benefits of living a life that aligns with His teachings, which assures paradise, and the consequences of straying from His path into damnation. It is a call to be mindful of the ultimate end, both in the present and in the end times, and to live one's life accordingly, maintaining awareness that this journey, our journey, is one toward returning to that from whence we've come.

Finally, the command to do both is not just for the individual, but also for the collective. It is a daily action that should not be forsaken, as it is for benefit of humanity as a whole. Ultimately, the goal is to gain approval from God, who has given this command for betterment of all creation.

This passage emphasizes the importance of aligning oneself with God's will and teachings in all aspects of life. It calls for a deep understanding of precepts left throughout the ages and a commitment toward living a life that aligns with them.

Reflective Question:

How can we apply the call to know God's statutes, keep His judgments, and do both in our daily lives?

Original Text:

When kept are His statutes and judgments, this action is equivalent to knowing one's purpose: to search for the sparks of light, wherever they may be, and raise them to holiness. Once all the sparks of the divine light have been collected, the vessels that once contained them will he restored.

Commentary:

The idea of searching for sparks of light and raising them to holiness comes from the Kabbalistic story of the shattering of the vessels and the scattering of the divine light. When we keep God's statutes and judgments, we are essentially on a mission to gather these sparks and restore the vessels that contain them. This means living a life that is aligned with God's will, seeking to bring light and goodness to the world, and actively working towards the restoration of all things.

This concept of searching for sparks of light is also connected to the idea of Tikkun Olam, or repairing the world. The Kabbalists believed that the world was originally created in a state of perfection but was shattered due to human error and sin. It is the responsibility of humans to work towards repairing this world by gathering the sparks of light and restoring the vessels that contain them.

The idea of seeking and restoring divine light can be a source of inspiration and motivation for individuals to live a purposeful and meaningful life. It can encourage us to strive towards goodness and righteousness in our daily actions, seeking to make the world a better place and bring healing to those who are suffering.

Reflective Question:

How can the concept of searching for sparks of divine light and working towards restoring the vessels that contain them inspire you to live a more purposeful and meaningful life?

Original Text:

Often is the evidence of God to provide a clear mapping of His expectation of man. This mapping painstakingly outlines the path to success, its boundaries are aligned with dignity and the knowledge that every step is a true orchestration of redemption that levels the playing field for achieving ones intended purpose for being here. It is the expectation of restoration that the righteous wait to rejoice in the return of the Messiah.

Commentary:

The statement reflects the idea that God has given humans a clear understanding of the expectations and purpose of their existence through various teachings and scriptures. The use of the word "mapping" suggests that God has created a clear path for humans to follow in order to achieve success and fulfill their intended purpose. This path is not arbitrary but is aligned with dignity and is an orchestration of redemption that levels the playing field for all to achieve their intended purpose.

The statement also alludes to the return of the Messiah, which is a significant event in many religious traditions. The expectation of restoration implies that the current state of humanity is incomplete and that the return of the Messiah will restore humanity to its intended state.

Reflective Question:

Do you believe that God has provided a clear path for humans to follow? How do you interpret the idea of a "path to success" in your own life? What does the concept of restoration mean to you personally?

Conclusion: Keep My Judgements and Do Them

The idea that God has provided a clear mapping of His expectations for humanity emphasizes the importance of seeking and following this path. It is a reminder that there is a purpose to our existence, and that purpose is aligned with dignity and the restoration of all things. This mapping is not arbitrary, but a true orchestration of redemption that levels the playing field for all to achieve their intended purpose. As we strive to follow this path and fulfill our purpose, we await the return of the Messiah and the ultimate restoration of all things.

Chapter 30

CONCLUSION

Within this journey of exponential thought and reflection, trusted is the prevalence of considerations heretofore unknown to the reader. Although the content may prove for many quite academic, it is the simplicity to take the topical selections and their applications to heart such that one's own conception, strength and understanding will manifest reality and enable self and others toward potentials heretofore unknown. For in this writing is an avenue most often taken for granted and/or plainly ignored, where reality filters the mind and experiences cultivate fruit anxious for presentation. Lost in the equation, however, is the will to move beyond the pages of this writing into one's own reality; a manifestation so profound that change in thought patterns and situational circumstances become a welcome guest to one's new reality, and the sounding board to aspirations heretofore unimaginable. It is within these implanted seeds that reality proports to manifest potential toward change, improvement, and/or generational expectations.

Thus, the challenge for the reader has been the opportunity for an inward evaluation of one's potential to explore, appreciate and manifest the reality of one's own thought in addressing, exploring or contemplating his/her role as specific in each of the topics ventured in this book; a writing that remained dormant for well over two decades as talent, time and tenacity opened the door necessary for a larger audience to receive benefit of this book's contents. For it is time that has thrust itself from the past into the present-era, and future generations to come. Even more is the magnitude of both "space and time" for readers' to cultivate consciousness of daily actions, common speech and fraternal relations such that passive appreciations become active applications in the presence of decent and/or moral behavior; the substance of the clarion call that resonates throughout the contents of this book.

Finally, and through benefit of this publication, trusted is much will be appreciated whether as a personal read or a group study; the hope being: reflection will breathe life into souls and hearts such that mindsets and attitudes are changed for the good.

Dr. Anna Lightfoot-Ward

Anna E. Lightfoot-Ward, Ph.D., has always been deeply rooted in her faith and education. Raised in a religious household, her spiritual upbringing played a significant role in shaping her values and ideals. Dr. Lightfoot-Ward's educational journey began at Florida International University, where she completed her Bachelor's and Master's degrees. Her passion for learning led her to the International Seminary, where she earned a Doctor of Philosophy degree.

Throughout her life, Dr. Lightfoot-Ward has consistently demonstrated a strong sense of community and civic duty. This commitment has been evident in her various roles, such as her time on the El Portal Village Council, where she served as Councilwoman and Mayor from 1994 to 1996. During her tenure, she focused on budget management, infrastructure improvements, and professionalizing the council's operations, all while fostering an atmosphere of decorum and respect.

Dr. Lightfoot-Ward's dedication to public service extends beyond her local community. As a United States Army veteran, she has displayed an unwavering commitment to her country. Her extensive educational background, including a Master's Degree in Public Administration, has equipped her with the skills necessary for effective city management. Between 1982 and 2002, Dr. Lightfoot-Ward held positions as assistant and deputy city manager in five medium and small cities. Additionally, she has shared her expertise as an adjunct professor at Miami Dade Community College.

A proud mother of three successful adult children and the loving wife of Dwight S. Garmon, Dr. Anna E. Lightfoot-Ward's life is a testament to the power of faith, education, and service in shaping an individual's journey and impact on the world.

Ingram Content Group UK Ltd.
Milton Keynes UK
UKHW021905020623
422807UK00006B/13

9 781088 129128